ANTIQUE OFFICE MACHINES:

600 Years of Calculating Devices

Thomas A. Russo

4880 Lower Valley Road, Atglen, PA 19310 USA

Copyright © 2001 by Thomas A. Russo
Library of Congress Card Number: 2001087586

All rights reserved. No part of this work may be reproduced or used in any form or by any means—graphic, electronic, or mechanical, including photocopying or information storage and retrieval systems—without written permission from the copyright holder.

"Schiffer," "Schiffer Publishing Ltd. & Design," and the "Design of pen and ink well" are registered trademarks of Schiffer Publishing Ltd.

Designed by "Sue"
Type set in Korinna BT

ISBN: 0-7643-1346-0
Printed in China
1 2 3 4

Published by Schiffer Publishing Ltd.
4880 Lower Valley Road
Atglen, PA 19310
Phone: (610) 593-1777; Fax: (610) 593-2002
E-mail: Schifferbk@aol.com
Please visit our web site catalog at **www.schifferbooks.com**
We are always looking for people to write books on new and related subjects. If you have an idea for a book please contact us at the above address.

This book may be purchased from the publisher.
Include $3.95 for shipping.
Please try your bookstore first.
You may write for a free catalog.

In Europe, Schiffer books are distributed by
Bushwood Books
6 Marksbury Ave.
Kew Gardens
Surrey TW9 4JF England
Phone: 44 (0) 20 8392-8585; Fax: 44 (0) 20 8392-9876
E-mail: Bushwd@aol.com
Free postage in the U.K., Europe; air mail at cost.

Contents

Acknowledgment 4

Preface 5

Chapter One: History of Counting 7

Chapter Two: Adding Machines, Calculator and Counters 13

Chapter Three: Combination Adding Machines and Cash Drawers ... 154

Chapter Four: Combination Adding Machines and Typewriters 169

Chapter Five: Slide Rules 178

Chapter Six: Electronic Calculators and Desktop Computers 197

Chapter Seven: Chronological Time Line 220

Bibliography 223

Index 224

Acknowledgment

As always, my wife and family have been the inspiration behind my desire to complete this book on calculating devices. They are always present, supporting, encouraging and congratulating.

The pictures in this book were taken by myself. Never having been a photography expert, I relied on the guidance and advice of the following individuals: Douglas Congdon-Martin, of Schiffer Publishing, and Nina Wolf, a professional photographer, and on assistance from my local camera shop, Camera's, Etc. With their combined help, my photographic efforts improved.

Part of the inspiration for this book came from wonderful friends and fellow employees at Remington Rand, who designed, promoted, sold, and serviced adding machines and calculators.

I would also like to express a special thanks to the collectors of calculating machines. As a result of our common interests and endeavors, I now count a number of them among my friends; in particular Larry Wilhelm, Conrad Schure, Bob Otnes, and many others.

And finally, my long time friend and associate, Sonya Zawalski who has helped with the typing, editing and formatting of this book.

Preface

The object of this book is to catalog some of those wonderful mechanical devices that were designed to help us through the laborious task of mathematical computations. For the most part these mechanical calculators were remarkably accurate. I always smile when I remember back to the early 1960s, while I was attending a management conference. The Branch Manager from Milwaukee, Wisconsin, Rick Rickets, was chosen to demonstrate to this conference of approximately 150-200 nationwide Remington management personnel and former salesmen, the new Remington Model 99120 printing calculator. His demonstration was a beautiful exercise of precision and was intended to guide the viewer's attention away from the slow and plodding cranking of the calculator.

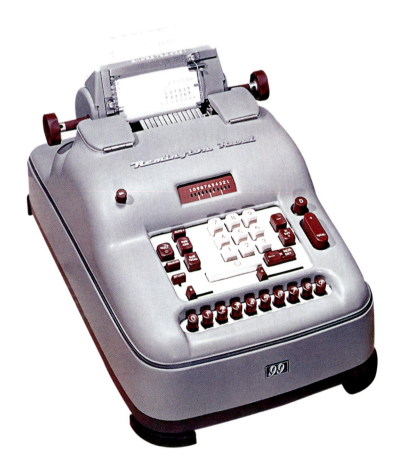

Remington Model 99120.

Rick indexed the full capacity of the machine and divided that by 999,999,999. Once he depressed the division key and the machine started its ponderous cycling, Rick very slowly took out a cigar from his suit coat pocket and equally slowly removed the wrapper from the cigar. By this time, everyone's attention was on Rick and not on the convulsions of the calculator. He then put the cigar in his mouth and slowly fumbled in his pockets for a lighter. Finally, he lit the cigar, inhaled, and slowly blew a perfect circle of smoke. Rick had timed all his actions to coincide precisely to end just as the calculator stopped its noisy cycling and finished the problem. Then Rick turned to the audience and commented, "Fast son of a gun, isn't it?"

It is hard to believe the instantaneous results of modern calculators. I marvel at how impatient we get with a desktop computer when it appears that the answer may take longer than a few seconds.

I have attempted to provide the reader with a value for these artifacts. But, these values are simply a guide and are based on the price the author paid for them or in some cases what they have sold for at auctions or private sales.

In the final analysis, price depends on availability, condition, appearance, and how badly the seller wants to sell and the buyer wants to buy.

Chapter One
History of Counting

Counting or the system of numbers that we call arithmetic, more than likely started in ancient times. No one knows for sure but there is some speculation that counting began by using fingers (*digitus*-Latin orig.) to identify one or more objects. For example, a number was given to each finger: one, two, three, four and up to ten. These whole (*integer*-Latin orig.) numbers are collectively referred to as **base ten**. The following chart is from the 1924 edition of *The American Digest of Business Machines,* which was compiled, edited and published by James H. McCarthy, Chicago.

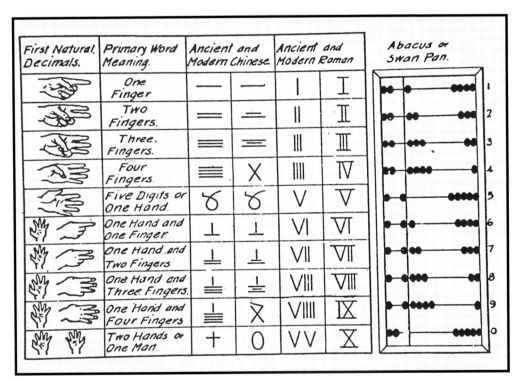

Chart illustrating the progression of the numbering system. *The American Digest of Business Machines.*

The chart above demonstrates the progression of the numbering system from fingers to the abacus. Note how the ancient numbering system of using fingers progressed to the Chinese and Roman systems. By holding a hand out and extending the index finger in a parallel manner, one can easily follow the above chart. This allows you to see how the Chinese advanced the numeral system. They wrote the number one as a parallel line to represent one finger; two parallel lines for two fingers; and three lines for three fingers, etc. The Roman system merely changed the parallel line to a vertical line.

Arabic numerals and the decimal system were the contributions of the Arabs who brought them from India. Both were found on the Rock Edicts of Ashoka (256 BC).

By the time history was first being recorded, mathematics was not only widely in use but also highly developed. In 2700 BC, the Egyptian architect, Imhotep, would have had a difficult time designing and building the pyramid at Saqqara without the use of mathematics. It is believed that multiplication tables and division were also in use at the time of the building of the pyramids.

A Jewish historian, Flavius Josephus, (circa 37-100 AD) believed that Abraham brought mathematics with him from the city of Ur in Chaldea to Egypt.

In 2000 BC Babylonian mathematics were said to have reached a high level with a sexagesimal system, which was based on the number sixty (60). The numbers one to six can be exactly divided into sixty. We can see this system in the use of sixty (60) seconds in a minute; sixty (60) minutes in an hour; three hundred and sixty (360) degrees in a circle, etc.

Will Durant in his book *Our Oriental Heritage, The Story of Civilization*, states that the Tasmanians counted up to two or "parmery, calabawa, cardia" which translated is "one, two, plenty." Durant further states that since counting was done by the use of fingers, the decimal system was born. Later someone thought of the idea of twelve, which was divisible by five of the first six whole numbers. From these beginnings sprang the duodecimal system (base 12) with twelve months in a year; twelve units in a dozen; twelve dozen in a gross; and twelve inches in a foot. The number thirteen (13) is not easily devisable and therefore was thought to be unlucky.

Later, in addition to fingers, counting was done using pebbles. The use of the *little stone,* (calculus) had many applications. A shepherd might use them to keep track of his herd. In the morning when he took the sheep to the pasture, he might drop one stone for each sheep in a basket or, possibly, a clay container. When he returned he would remove one stone from the pile for each sheep found until he had accounted for them all.

Later these stones or pebbles were arranged in rows and could be moved back and forth along lines in the dust. Still later, lines were ruled on stone, wood, or marble tablets. In 1300 BC, a device that resembles what we today would call an *abacus* appeared in China.

A Chinese *abacus* (*souanpan* or *swan pan,* which translates to "counting board"*)*, could best be described as an instrument made of wood, pebbles, or beads, and rods or wires. It consisted of a frame, rectangular in shape, that joined a number of wires or rods together on which beads could be moved back and forth. The rods were divided into two sections of unequal length. The lower or larger section had five beads and the upper or smaller section had two beads. Each column represented a decimal unit. Column one: units; column two: tens; column three: hundreds, and so on. The abacus was ingenious in its simplicity and in the hands of a skilled operator has proven to be much faster than calculating by hand with pencil and paper. In fact, it has been reported that in some cases it was faster than many mechanical adding or calculating machines. The *abacus* has had a remarkably long life and is still used today in some parts of the world.

An important event in the development of our system of mathematics was the discovery and use of the "zero." In Michael R. Williams' wonderful book, *A History of Computing Technology*, (Prentice-Hall, Inc., Englewood Cliffs, New Jersey, 1985*)*, we learn that the "zero" appeared as early as 200 BC. But it was not used as a part of their mathematical system. It was used only to represent an empty column. It is not known exactly when the "zero" became a part of our system of numbers as we use it today.

John Napier, (1550-1617) a Scottish mathematician, in his work, *Mirifici Logarithms Canonis Descriptio*, defined "an explanation of the nature of logarithms and of their use in numeration and in trigonometry." In addition to logarithms, Napier also invented the notation of decimal fractions.

Napier is most commonly known for his invention of "Napier's Bones." In 1617 he published *Rabdologia* (numeration by little rods), in which he describes these little rods as made of ivory or bone. Multiplication, division, extraction of square and cube root could all be performed by manipulation of the little rods. It was considered a great time saver during that period.

In 1623, Wilhelm Schickard (1592-1635) invented and built the first mechanical calculator. It is reported that he made two machines, one was destroyed by fire and the other disappeared after his death. Only his drawings remain. Over the years, reproductions have been made using Schickard's drawings as a guide; and one such device was given to the author as a gift by William Korsch in 1997, and is pictured below.

A nineteen-year old French mathematician, Blaise Pascal (1623-1662), produced the first truly mechanical calculator. Pascal's machine is called a calculator, but it is really an adding machine. Although multiplication is possible, it is complicated and is definitely not "automatic." It has been reported that a surprising number of machines still exist, but the author is only aware of a few.

Reproduction of Wilhelm Schickard's Mechanical Calculator

Thomas deColmar Calculator

During the next one hundred and fifty years, many adding machine and calculator inventions surfaced from all over the world. But it was not until 1820 that another Frenchman, Charles Xavier Thomas deColmar (1785-1870), would produce the world's first commercially successful four-function calculator that was not only practical but rapid. However, it was not completely automatic in that multiplication was accomplished through repeat addition. The Thomas machine was considered successful and from 1821 to 1870, he personally managed the factory in which machines were produced for distribution all over the world.

The model pictured is part of the author's collection and is one of the first one thousand calculators that Thomas manufactured. It has a serial number of 725, which means that it was probably manufactured sometime between 1865 and 1870.

Leon Bollée (1870-1913), a Frenchman, who having attained the age of 18, accomplished what no one before him, had done. He invented a mechanical solution to the direct multiplication problem. All machines before him used repeat addition in order to multiply, but Bollée found a way to short cut that process in 1889.

Otto Steiger patented what would become the world's first successful fully-automatic, four-function calculator. It was called the "Millionaire," and was manufactured by Hans W. Egli of Zurich, Switzerland.

The Millionaire calculator came with either levers on the earlier ones, (called the slide-board models) or more modern key-tops on the later ones, (called the keyboard models). It was available in a hand crank machine or in an electric version with an outboard motor under the main construction. Although the hand crank or manual model was advertised as portable, it weighed over 70 pounds. The electric model weighed even more.

Above and left:
The Millionaire

"Comptometer." It was fast, accurate, and its ease of operation was theretofore unmatched. The principle of Felt's machine was a live keyboard. Depressing the key, as opposed to using a hand crank, activated the mechanisms. On conventional adding machines, the operator had to first enter the amount on the keyboard by depressing the keys, then hand crank the lever, usually on the right side of the machine, which would enter or input these numbers. The operator had to either double crank the machine or depress a separate total key and; then, crank the machine again for a total. One can easily see why the Comptometer with its live keyboard was so successful.

The Comptometer that is pictured below is the first model introduced for sale. It had wood sides as opposed to later machines that were metal.

A lighter and smaller calculator was on the horizon. An American, Frank Stephen Baldwin (1838-1925), introduced to the world a new mechanical "pinwheel" principle that would allow for smaller, faster, and lighter calculators. Baldwin filed for a patent on October 5, 1892 and for an improvement on September 8, 1893.

Another American, Dorr E. Felt (1862-1930) developed an extremely successful calculator called the

Comptometer. Serial number: 408.

It is not surprising that someone would eventually attempt to develop a calculator that would do more than add, subtract, multiply and divide.

The man of the hour was Charles Babbage (1791-1871). Babbage had become an excellent mathematician and eventually a mechanic of the first order. His inspiration for the development of a "Difference Engine" came after reviewing a chart of mathematical tables in which he noted several errors. With the help of an initial grant from the British government, he began what was to become a long, unsuccessful attempt to complete his "Difference Engine." Although, Babbage was not able to enjoy the fruits of his creativeness, he did leave the world a complete set of drawings.

In 1833, Babbage envisioned a machine, that he called his "Analytical Engine." It was the germ of an idea that was to evolve into the modern computer. His analytical engine would have a *"store"* or memory; a *"mill,"* or number crunching or arithmetic processing unit; an *"output,"* or printout mechanism; and an *"input"* device in which a form of punch cards would be used. The latter was an inspiration that Babbage conceived after seeing a portrait of "Joseph Marie Jacquard" that was woven with different colors of silk thread. The portrait was done to demonstrate the application of punch cards to automatically produce the picture.

The British government decided to discontinue funding the Babbage engine and although Babbage tried to finish the analytical engine on his own, he finally gave up. He knew he would be unable to finish it before his death.

In 1993, an interesting article written by Doron D. Swade appeared in the February issue of the *Scientific American Magazine*, published by Scientific American, Inc. of New York. Swade was not only an electronic engineer and a historian of computers, but also the senior curator at the Science Museum in London. In 1985, he and several of his colleagues, using Babbage's drawings, set out to complete the construction of the "Difference Engine No. 2" and once and for all determine if it would do what over 150 years previously, Babbage had claimed it would. In 1991, the project was finally completed and the mechanical device that they called the "Difference Engine No. 2" performed the tasks as was originally claimed. Babbage had designed the world's first mechanical computer.

The Remington Rand Corporation delivered its first electronic computer to the United States Census Bureau in 1951. It was called "Univac." Surprisingly, Remington Rand executives felt that there was not a very big market for their computer and thought they might sell six or seven Univac machines per year. At the time of this writing, Univac is part of the Unisys Corporation.

The Bell Punch Company, Ltd. of London, England patented the world's first electronic desk calculator in 1958 under the British patent number 868,753-19656/58. Later it was patented in the United States under the United States patent number 682,376. It was called the "Anita" calculator. The Anita calculator pictured below is from the author's collection and has serial and model number, C/VIII/014092AA.

Anita Electronic Calculator

During the last half of the 1970s, special application computers, especially for word processing became an overnight success. Companies such as IBM, Wang, Xerox, CPT, Vydec, and Redactron were all represented with competitive products. Credit for coining the phrase "word processing" belongs to IBM. Their introduction of the IBM Magnetic Tape Typewriter in the late 1950s allowed typists to store information on magnetic tape for repetitive letters and editing. Later these machines were available to accommodate various kinds of magnetic media, i.e., magnetic cards and floppy disks.

Word processing was the primary application that launched the microprocessor desktop computer, especially to private industry. In 1974, Xerox produced the first personal computer. It was called the "Alto," but was never sold commercially.

From the mid to late 1970s, Apple, Commodore, Tandy (Radio Shack) and others were marketing desktop computers. Xerox finally entered the market with a 1973 CP/M based operating system. By 1982 the Victor Adding Machine Company, a subsidiary of Kidde, Inc., released the Victor 9000 CP/M based desktop computer. It was considered to be the state of the art for CP/M based systems for that period as the following chart will attest:

Make & Model	Victor 9000	IBM PC	Apple III	Apple Model II	Radio Shack TRS80
Processor Type	8088	8088	Z80A	6502	Z80A
Word Length	16 bits	16 bits	8 bits	8 bits	8 bits
Memory Size					
Internal	128-896KB	16-256KB	64KB	96-256KB	32-64KB
Storage Capacity on 2 Floppies	2400KB (5 ¼")	640KB (5 ¼")	184KB (5 ¼")	280KB (5 ¼")	960KB (8")
CRT Display					
Standard Format	80 x 25	80 x 25	80 x 24	80 x 24	80 x 24
Alternate Format	132 x 50	None	None	None	None
Graphics Resolution	800 x 400	840 x 200	None	None	None
Communications					
Built-in Serial Ports at no extra cost	2	0	2	1	2
Built-in Parallel Ports at no extra cost	1	0	2	0	1
Human Factors					
Keys on Keyboard	94-104	83	96	74	76
Detached Keyboard	Yes	Yes	Yes	No	No
Tilting Design mechanism	Yes	No	No	No	No
Swiveling Display mechanism	Yes	No	No	No	No
Desk Area Required (Approx. Square in. with 2 floppy disks)	310	420	470	361	500
Operating System Supplied Standard	CP/M-86 MS-DOS	None	None	Apple DOS	TRS DOS

NOTE: Chart based on manufacturer's advertising of information from "Dataquest, Inc." available as of April 4, 1962.

But in 1981, the PC-DOS version 1.0 operating system was released along with the IBM's 5150 personal computer. Two years later IBM followed up with a newer model called the 5160 PC XT. The design and technology of the personal computer made possible look-a-like products that were called clones. Dozens of clone manufacturers sprang up over night. A highly competitive and volatile market developed with the United States taking a commanding worldwide lead.

From the advent of the earliest abacus to Schickard's first calculator to Babbage's first mechanical computer to today's desktop computer, took almost six hundred years of man's inventive genius, struggles and accomplishments. How fortunate we are to live in a period where the world has shrunk to the size of the Internet and mail is instantaneous. A time when information, libraries, encyclopedias, world shopping, news and weather are at our fingertips and available upon demand. Yes, it is a wonderful time to be alive, but there are those of us who will always cherish the history and artifacts of the men whose genius and tenacity are responsible for the world we live in today.

Chapter Two
Adding Machines, Calculators, and Counters

Abacus. Japanese *soroban*, first appeared 16th century.

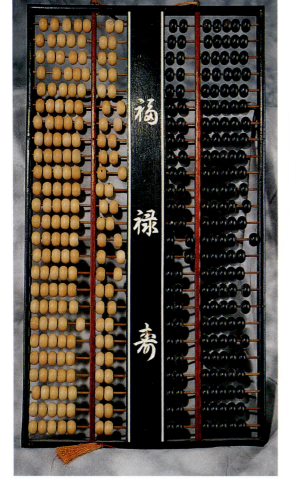

Abacus. Chinese *swan pan (or souanpan)*, first appeared 13th century.

Abacus. Russian *stchoty*, first appeared 17th century.

14　Addac

Addac. Manufactured by the Addac Company, Houseman Building in Grand Rapids, Michigan. The Addac had a short life span. It was placed on the market in 1926 and discontinued in 1928. It is not known how many were actually manufactured, but based on the two years it was in existence, the Addac should be considered at least scarce. It was a non-listing machine with eight place settings. To add, the operator pulled the lever on the right side of the machine down. To subtract, the lever was pushed up. The serial number of the machine pictured is 01,369. Dimensions: 5.50" h x 8" w x 4.50" d. Availability: Scarce. Value: $200.

Add-Em. Manufactured by the Tom Thumb, Western Stamping Company of Jackson, Michigan. The Add-Em adding machine was a child's toy adder and added from 1 to 999. There are only three (3) keys. To add a series of numbers, the instructions direct the operator to push each key twice to register 222. To add 321 to that figure, you were instructed to push the number 1 key once, then push the number 2 key twice, and finally the number 3 key three times. This accumulated total was 543. Dimensions: 3" h x 5" w x 9.5" long. Availability: Common. Value: $10.

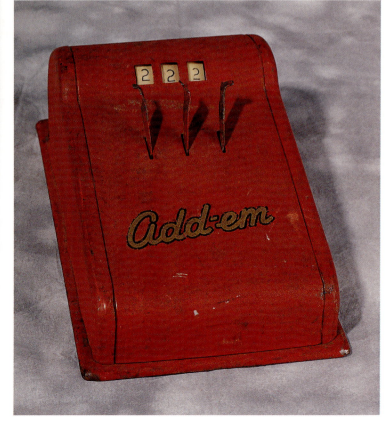

Add-A-Skill. Manufactured by the Add-A-Skill Company of Pilot Point, Texas. This was one of the many teaching aid products developed to help operators increase their speed. With practice and using the ten-key touch method, an operator could attain a high degree of proficiency. Dimensions: 2" h x 5" w x 7" long. Availability: Common. Value: $10.

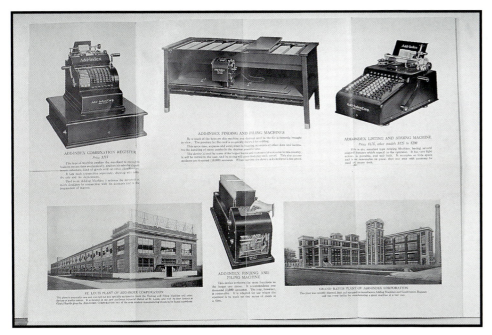

Above and right:
Add-Index. A later model of the electric Add-Index. (c.1922) It was considered to be a portable and was also manufactured by the Add-Index Corporation of Grand Rapids, Michigan. It used either AC or DC voltage. The pictured unit is a Model 1099 with serial number: 316,654. Availability: Scarce. Value: $150.

Adder, The. *See Webb Adder*

Adder, the (cardboard). Invented and copyrighted by Jowell Brothers of Newark, New Jersey. This little cardboard adder had five circular dials or wheels with an arrow in the center of each. The first wheel on the right is units; the second tens; the third hundreds, and so on. The answer appeared in the five openings on back of the card. Dimensions: 7.125" w x 4" long. Availability: Scarce. Value: $15.

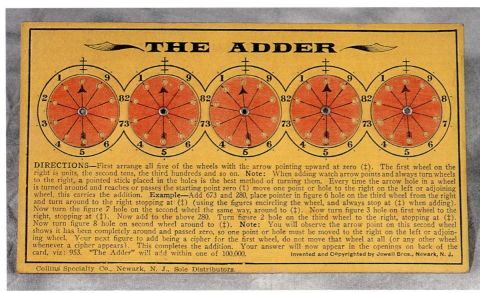

16 Addiator

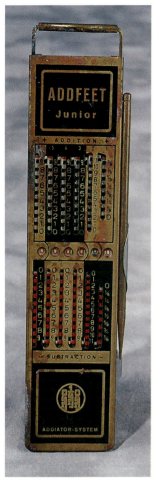

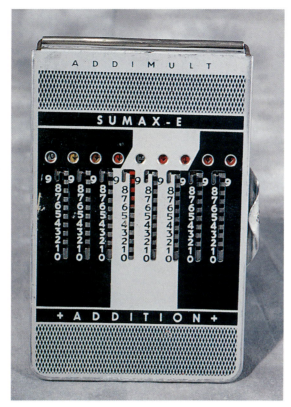

Addimult (Sumax-E). A vertical slide cogged bar adder that does addition on the front side and subtraction on the reverse. Made in Western Germany. Availability: Common. Value: $5.

Addiator (Addfeet Junior). One of the many so-called Addiator Systems, a foot and inch adding machine. Availability: Common. Value: $10.

Addiator (Fractomator). This version of the Addiator was manufactured by the Addimax Addiator Company in Western Germany. It is a feet and inches adder of the stylus-type. Addition is performed on the front of the machine and subtraction on the back or reverse side. Serial number: D-805,760. Availability: Scarce. Value: $125.

Above and right:
Adding Machine. There are two models of the Adding Machine. One was a toy and manufactured by the Dayton Friction Toy Company of Dayton, Ohio. It had an orange colored metal case. The other had a wood case and was manufactured by the Kel-San Manufacturing Company also of Dayton, Ohio. The patent number on both machines is 1,663,726 (c.1928). Availability: Common. Value: Each: $75.

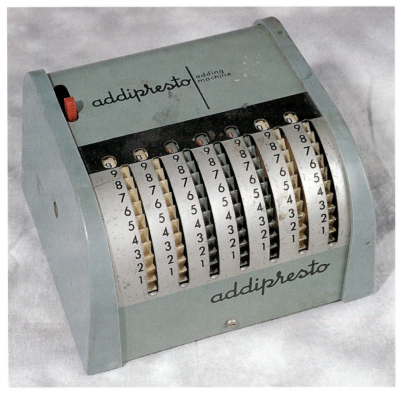

Addipresto. This small stylus-type adder was manufactured in Italy, (Brevetti Lanza-Savona). Dimensions: 3.5" h x 6" w x 5.125" d. Availability: Common. Value: $10.

Add-O-Matic

Add-O-Matic. Manufactured by the Allied Manufacturing Company of Chicago, Illinois. The directions indicate that the Add-O-Matic could add, subtract, multiply, and divide. It had lever-type keys and a "figures" pointer in which the larger figures were used for addition and multiplication and the small figures for subtraction. The results appeared in the five place windows at the bottom of the machine. Dimensions: 4.5" h x 5" w x 11" long. Availability: Common. Value: $125.

Below:
Addometer. Manufactured by the Reliable Typewriter & Adding Machine Corporation of Chicago, Illinois. The Addometer is a wheel and stylus-type adder and is rectangular in shape. It was simple to use. The operator merely turned the wheels to the right to add (using large figures) and to subtract turn left (using small figures). The first model (pictured) came in a case and it was designed to be used as a ruler and line finder simply by being laid on top of the figures to be input. The second model was a desk model and came with a wood base that placed the adder at a 45-degree angle. One edge of the adder was an 11" ruler. The clearing mechanism and the stylus are on the right side of the adder. Dimensions: 11.5" w x 2.375" h. Availability: Common. Value: $25.

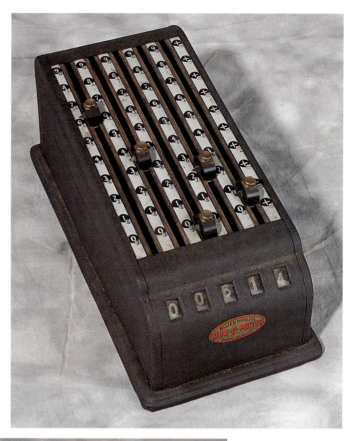

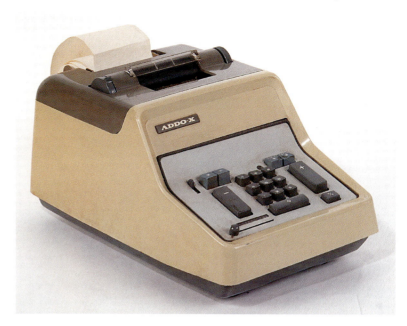

Addo-X (Model 2383). An electrically operated ten-key keyboard unit. Made in Sweden. Assigned United States patent numbers were: 2,715,496; 2,946,507 and 2,985,363. Availability: Common. Value: $25.

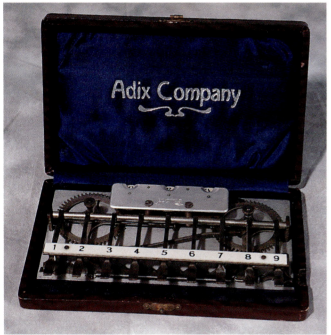

Adix. A very unique adding device. All of the mechanism is exposed. Availability: Scarce. Value: $400.

Allen, R. C. (Model 67). Manufactured by the R. C. Allen Business Machines Company of Grand Rapids, Michigan. A full-keyboard hand-operated adder. Serial number: 1,348,380. Availability: Common. Value: $25.

Allen, R. C. (Model 35). This model was called the "World Famos." Serial number: 32,851. Availability: Scarce. Value: $125.

Allen, R. C. (Model 75-10). A 10-key listing, hand-operated adding machine. Serial number: 1,514,990. Availability: Common. Value: $35.

AMCO. Manufactured by the Accounting Machine Company of New York, New York. It is a seven place setting machine. To operate, the finger is placed on the figure desired and pushed down to the stop. This in turn registers the number. The seven red keys at the top of the adder are used for subtraction. The company was sold to the Todd Protectograph Company and placed on the market as the Starr Adding Machine. Dimensions: 5.75" h x 5.375" w x 6.375" long. Serial number: 8,315. Availability: Common. Value: $25.

American (Model 1). Manufactured by the American Can Company of Chicago, Illinois. Later it was manufactured and sold by the American Adding Machine Company, 35 South Dearborn Street of Chicago, Illinois. According to the "Business Machines and Equipment Digest," it was placed on the market in 1922 and in 1928 was still being sold. It must have been a very popular machine as they can easily be found at various antique marketplaces. The machine was activated by a unique finger action. The operator placed their index finger on the figure they desired and then placed the thumb of the same hand on the lever directly below. They then lifted the lever until it touched the index finger. Serial number: 12,926. Availability: Common. Value: $75.

American (Model 4). This was a printer or paper tape model. It was also used on a cash drawer as a Combination Cash Register. Availability: Scarce. Value: $75 - $150.

American (Model 5). A non-printing model, which listed 7 columns and totaled 8 columns. Availability: Common. Value: $25 - $50.

22 Archimedes

Archimedes (Model C). Manufactured by Fisher and Pöthig of Glashütte, Saxony. This is a stepped drum calculating arithmometer introduced in 1906. The Model C is sometimes called the Baby Archimedes since it is smaller than previous models. It has 10 setting slides, 16 places in the result register, and 9 in the revolution counter. Just above the setting slides are 10 windows used for error checking the setting slides. Serial number: 3,710. Availability: Scarce. Value: $2,000.

Argos (Model II). Manufactured by Gesellschaft Für Präzionstechnik G.m.b.H., Berlin, Germany. This was a small palm size adder that was chain set. It was introduced in 1913 and due to World War I, had a short life span;+ as a result, not many were made. Availability: Rare. Value: $800.

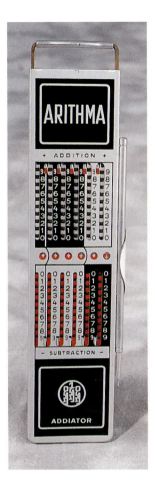
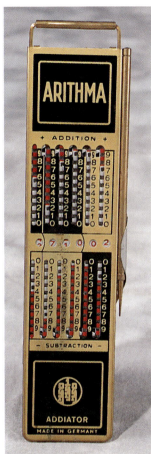

Arithma. Manufactured in West Germany (c.1940-1950). A stylus-operated, hand-held adding and subtracting device that sold originally for only $3.98. It was available in both silver and gold. Dimensions: 1.5" w x 6" long. Availability: Common. Value: $10.

Arithstyle. Manufactured by Gesellschaft für Maschinenbau und elektrische Neuheiten G.m.b.H., Berlin, Germany. The Arithstyle was first introduced in 1906. It was a nine-place, palm size, chain set adder. Availability: Rare. Value: $1,000.

24 Arrow

Arrow. Manufactured by the Arrow Calculating Manufacturing Company of New York, New York. The Arrow was introduced in 1921 and utilized the pinwheel principle that was first developed by Baldwin. Availability: Scarce. Value: $300.

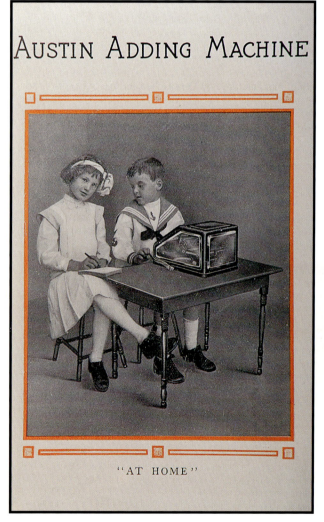

Left and below:
Austin. Manufactured by the Austin Adding Machine Corporation at 927 Linden Avenue in Baltimore, Maryland. The Austin is a lineal ten-key keyboard and nonprinting adding machine. The mechanism of the Austin was completely visible since the sides as well as the front and top of the machine were glass. Not many were manufactured. Availability: Rare. Value: $1,500.

Automatic Adding Machine Company. see Golden Gem and Gaucher.

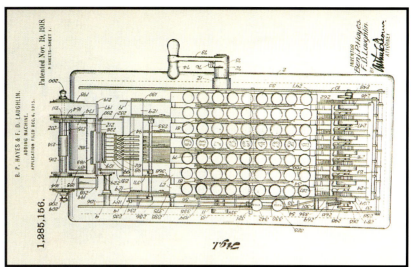

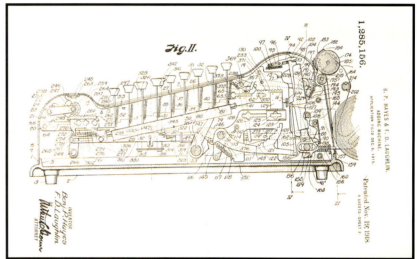

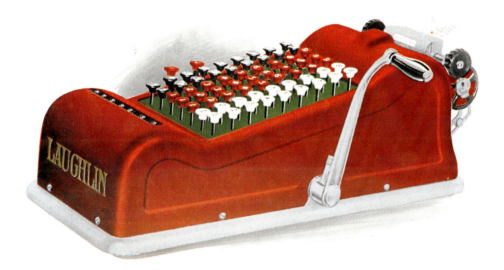

Automatic (Laughlin). Manufactured by the Automatic Bookkeeping Register Company at 18th and Wyandotte in Kansas City, Missouri. This is the company that had previously manufactured a *three hundred-pound* combination bookkeeping, adding, and cash register machine with little success. The president of the company was Frank D. Laughlin. Laughlin and Benjamin P. Hayes, an employee and mechanical whiz, applied for and received on November 19, 1918, United States patent number 1,285,156. Above is a concept rendering of the adding machine that was conceived. To my knowledge it was never produced.

Automatic

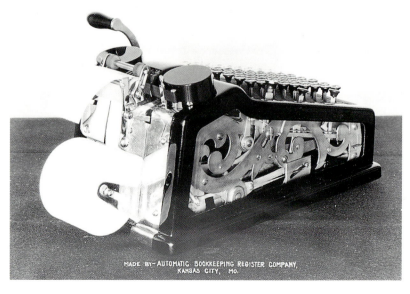

This adding machine has a serial number of 1 and was found by the author in the abandoned factory of the Automatic Bookkeeping Register Company in Kansas City, Missouri in 1997. This was either the patent model or the prototype. The company had elected to go into receivership and their doors were locked in 1923. Eventually the building was condemned and all the contents were auctioned off in 1997. The production model is shown in the pictured brochure. Availability: One of a kind. Value: $5,000 +.

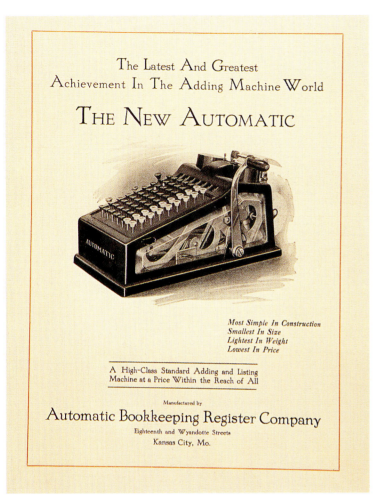

Automatic Adding Machine Production Model.

Baby Calculator. Stylus-operated with a "cogged vertical" slide bar for addition and subtraction. The manufacturer claimed it was also capable of multiplication and division. Made in Chicago, Illinois. Availability: Common. Value: $5.

Bair-Fulton

Bair-Fulton Calculator. Manufactured by the Bair-Fulton Company of York, Pennsylvania. This was a stylus-operated, cogged wheel-type device similar to the Lightning Adding Machine. The model number indicated the column capacity as can be seen in the following machines.

Bair-Fulton Calculator (Model 6). A six column, cogged wheel adder. Availability: Common. Value: $25.

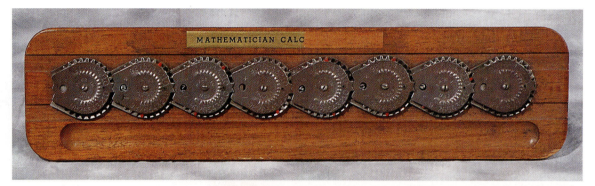

Bair-Fulton Calculator (Model 8). Eight column version. Availability: Common. Value: $25.

Bair-Fulton Calculator (Model 11). Availability: Rare. Value: $175.

Baldwin

The inventor of the Baldwin calculator and the pinwheel mechanical principle was Frank Stephen Baldwin. Baldwin was not only a creative inventor but very productive as well. During his lifetime he invented:

(1) a *coupler* for railroad cars in 1855;
(2) a *corn planting* machine in 1860;
(3) a *metal lace latch* for more quickly lacing shoes in 1869;
(4) a wind instrument called an *anemometer*;
(5) a *registering step* for street cars that recorded the number of passengers carried as well as;
(6) a *street indicator* that displayed the current street;
(7) a *recording lumber measurer* that automatically measured and recorded the board feet of lumber and took four different calculations.

Frank Stephen Baldwin (1838-1925)

Above and left:
The **Recording Lumber Measurer** pictured below, is the patent model, which was sent along with Baldwin's drawings to the Patent Office. It is reported to have given Baldwin the idea of another calculator utilizing a different mechanical principle called the "variable tooth gear." Availability: One of a kind. Value: $8,000.

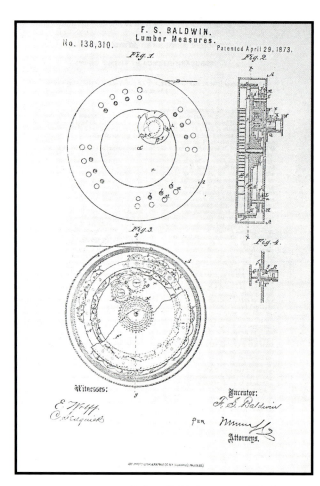 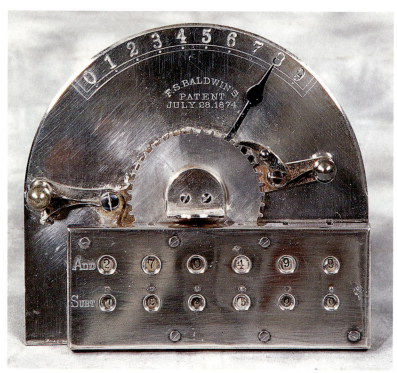

Before Baldwin patented his famous calculator, he patented a small adding machine. He called it an Arithmometer and also an Accountant's Assistant. It was issued patent number 153,522 dated July 28, 1874. Availability: Rare. Value: $9,000.

Inside the original box of the Arithmometer is an eleven-page combination brochure and instruction booklet. The booklet shows all three Baldwin devices: including the Lumber Measurer; the Arithmometer, and his first calculator.

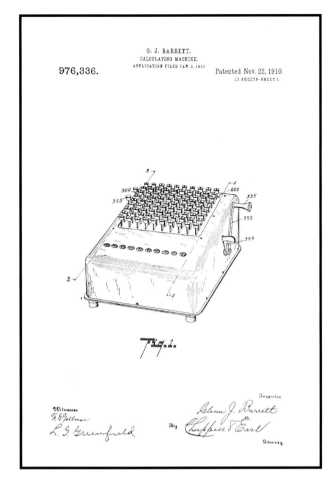
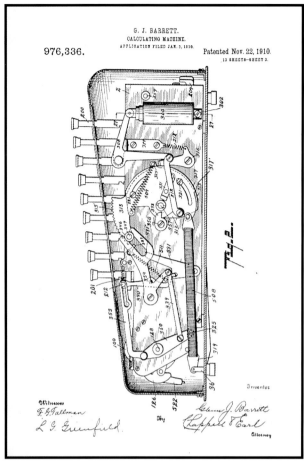

Barrett Adding Machine. The inventor of the Barrett adding machine was Glen G. Barrett of Grand Rapids, Michigan. United States patent number 976,336 dated November 22, 1910 was issued and production began a few years later. Early models were supplied with a "Mezzanine" attachment. This allowed entered figures to be repeated as well as shifted into the next column automatically. Availability: Common. Value: $125.

Barrett Advertising. showing models 6, 10, and 12.

Barrett (Model 2). Manufactured by the Barrett Adding Machine Company of Grand Rapids, Michigan. This model was a full-keyboard, non-printing adder. Serial number: 6,454. (c.1912) Availability: Common. Value: $150.

Barrett (Model 12). Manufactured by the Barrett Adding Machine Company of Philadelphia, Pennsylvania. A full-keyboard printer. Serial number: 11,249. Patent date: April 16, 1912. Availability: Common. Value: $75.

Barrett (Model A). Manufactured by the Lanston Monotype Machine Company of Philadelphia, Pennsylvania. Serial number: A10,138. Availability: Common. Value: $50.

Above and right:
Bassett. A continuous band stylus-operated adder manufactured by the J. H. Bassett Company of Chicago, Illinois. (c.1909-1930) Availability: Scarce. Value: $125.

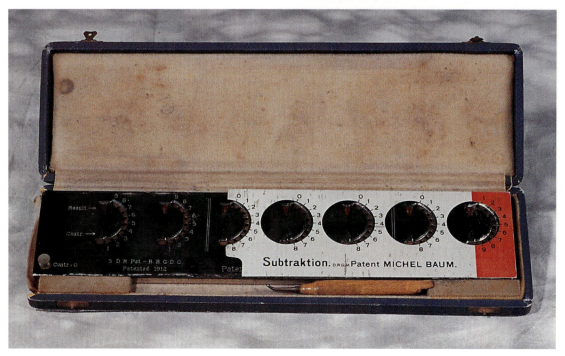

Baum, Michel. A stylus-type adder using a semi-circle for each column. For example, a seven-column adder would have seven semi-circles laid out horizontally on a ruler-like base. A separate tin cover slides over the unit for use when subtracting. First appeared around 1913. Availability: Scarce. Value: $150.

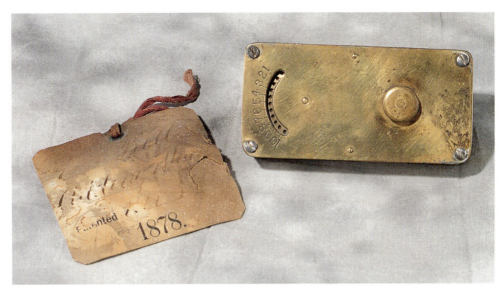

Right and below:
Bill. The patent model by Edward L. Bill of Wheeling, West Virginia. Patent number: 209,644 dated November 5, 1878. Referred to by the inventor as an improvement in calculators or adding machines, this device provided the exchange rate of currency between England and America or from pounds and shillings to dollars and cents. It is not known if this device was ever placed on the market. Availability: Rare. Value: $4,500.

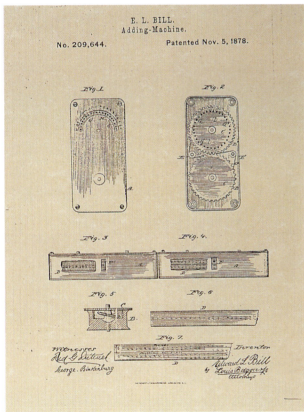

Bri-Cal. Manufactured by the British Calculators Limited of Stoke Newington, London N., England. It is a circular, hand-held, stylus-operated adding machine produced in 1905. Availability: Scarce. Value: $500.

36 Britannic

Britannic. Manufactured by Guy's Calculating Machines Limited, Truro Works, Wood Green, London, England. This was a brass clone of the typical pinwheel-type calculator. (c.1922) Availability: Scarce. Value: $400.

Brunsviga - Manufactured by the Grimme, Natalis and Co. A. G. of Braunschweig, Germany. This popular calculator followed the basic design of the original Odhner machine with a few added improvements. It first appeared in 1892 and had a long and successful career. Carl H. Reuter, Inc. of Philadelphia, Pennsylvania distributed the Brunsviga in the United States. Many models were available and a few are in the author's collection. Availability: Common. Value: $250.

Brunsviga (Model Trinks). Manufactured by the Grimme Natalis Company A.G. Germany. The first model appeared on the market about 1892. This firm acquired the patent from the Original Odhner and made substantial improvements that resulted in the Brunsviga. Serial number: 12,186. United States patent date: January 11, 1910. Availability: Scarce. Value: $400.

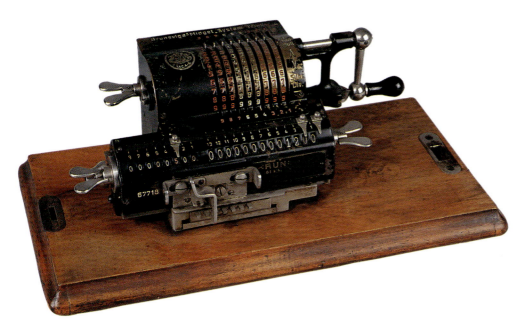

Brunsviga Midget. A smaller version of the pinwheel type calculator. Availability: Common. Value: $300.

Brunsviga Nova (Model 11). Serial number of the machine pictured is 6T20,700. Availability: Common. Value: $225.

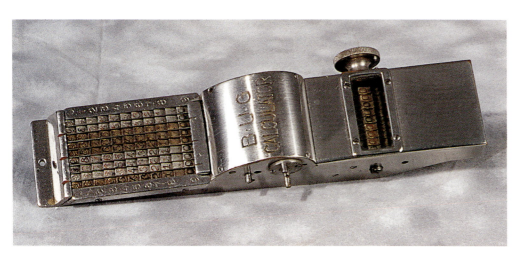

BUC. Manufactured by the Bergman Universal Company. Serial number: 2,971. Availability: Scarce. Value: $400.

Burkhardt (Model H). Invented by Arthur Burkhardt in 1878. It was based on the stepped drum principle generally attributed to Thomas de Colmar. Burkhardt is considered the father of the calculator industry in Germany. The Burkhardt Arithmometer pictured has a serial number of 782,501. Availability: Rare. Value: $5,500.

Burroughs

Burrough's factory.

William Seward Burroughs (January 28, 1857 to September 14, 1898) was the inventor of the first Burroughs adding machine and the founder of the American Arithmometer Company in 1886. Born in Rochester, New York to a poor family, Burroughs was only able to finish elementary school.

By the time he was twenty years old, he managed to secure a job as a bookkeeper in a local bank. It was during this period that it occurred to Burroughs that a great deal of his time was wasted because of the need to slowly and carefully input his figures to prevent costly errors and almost as much time to proof his work. He knew there had to be a better way.

Burroughs' health had never been good and as a result his doctor recommended that he change occupations and climate.

THE BOYER MACHINE SHOP, ST. LOUIS, WHERE ONE OF THE FIRST SUCCESSFUL ADDING AND LISTING MACHINES WAS BORN
Courtesy of the Burroughs Adding Machine Company.

Boyer's Machine Shop

After relocating to the midwestern part of the United States, Burroughs took a job in a machine shop working for Frank S. Baldwin who was famous for his invention of the pinwheel calculating machine. It was during this time that Burroughs conceived the idea of an adding machine that would add columns. It was never clear whether Dorr E. Felt, inventor of the Felt & Tarrant Calculator, or Burroughs developed the first adding machine. Although Burroughs filed his application for a patent a year and a half earlier than Felt; Felt's patent was awarded in 1887, a year earlier than Burroughs was awarded his.

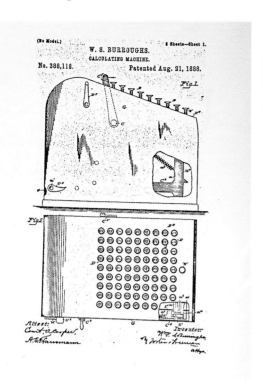 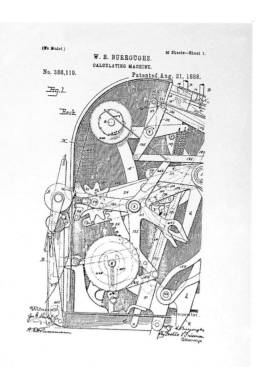

Burroughs Patents, Numbers 388,118 and 388,119 dated August 21, 1888.

Although his first machine was publicly exhibited in 1884, Burroughs did not secure his first patent until 1888. The basis for his initial patent was the "pivot" and it was the first of its kind granted for a key-set recording and adding machine.

There were so many complaints surrounding the operation of the hand crank that Burroughs scrapped the first 50 machines built and designed a new mechanism called, "Automatic Control." This feature insured that regardless of how hard or how easily the operator pulled the adding machine crank, there was no mechanical failure.

Although initial sales were slow, by 1895 sales increased to the point that manufacturing moved to a new and larger site in St. Louis, Missouri. It was just three years later that Burroughs died on Sept. 14, 1898. He did not live long enough to see the phenomenal success of the company that he founded.

Burroughs Plant (c.1913)

In 1904, the entire Burroughs plant was relocated to Detroit, Michigan. In 1911, the Pike Adding Machine Company patents were transferred to Burroughs enabling the company to announce their first visible adding and subtracting machine. In 1921, Burroughs acquired the Moon-Hopkins Billing Machine Company, giving Burroughs their first bookkeeping machine. By 1926, Burroughs had sold their one millionth (1,000,000th) adding machine.

Burroughs became one of the premier American corporations and survived hundreds of competitors, not to mention: a Civil War; World Wars I and II; the financial panics of 1873 and 1893; the stock market crash of 1929, and the subsequent Great Depression.

In 1985, sales grew to over five billion dollars per year. But perhaps it was after Burroughs built a memory device for ENIAC, the world's first electronic digital computer in 1952, that the future direction of the company became clear. After years of aborted attempts to gain a greater share of the computer market, a merger with Univac, the computer giant of Blue Bell, Pennsylvania was completed. The two companies became known as Unisys.

Left and below:
Burroughs Class 1 (Model 6) – This was an early printing adding machine. (c.1909) It was called a blind model because the operator could not see the printed results since the mechanism was located at the lower rear part of the machine. Serial number: 133,277. Availability: Common. Value: $125.

42 Burroughs

This page:
Burroughs Class 3 (Model 301). This is a 5 list and 6 total adding machine. It has a repeat key for use in multiplication and division and a non-add key which enables the operator to enter dates, clerk identifications and voucher numbers. Serial number: 628,696. Availability: Common. Value: $50.

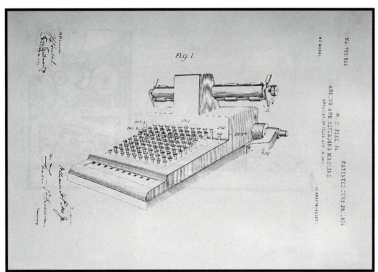

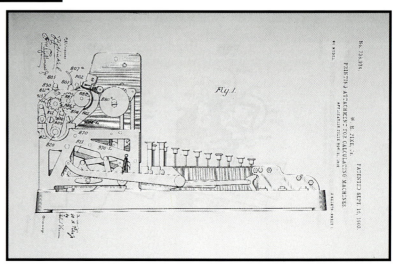

Burroughs Class 4. Equipped with a feature called the "Multiplying Keyboard." This was a lever that moved the multiplicand from right to left and left to right, while multiplying. Serial number: 1,361,351. Availability: Common. Value: $75.

Left and above:
Burroughs Class 8 (Portable). This 1925 model had completely new mechanical and cosmetic designs. As a result it was much lighter than the Class 3 machines. Serial number: 63,486. Availability: Common. Value: $150.

44 Burroughs

Burroughs Class 5 (Model A). A key-driven, 5 column, hand-operated calculator. Serial number: 375,244. Availability: Common. Value: $75.

Burroughs Class 5 (Model A-High Profile Version). A key-driven calculator. Serial number: 342,692. Availability: Common. Value: $150.

Burroughs Class 5 (Model 5205). A key-driven, non-printing, 9 column, high-speed calculator. Serial number: 494,644. Availability: Common. Value: $150.

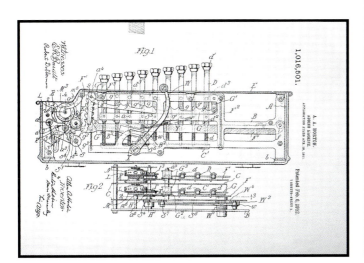 

Burroughs Class 5 (Model 520). New style version of the Model 5205 shown previously. It is an identical copy of the Felt & Tarrant calculator. Serial number: 207,150 with United States patent dates: February 6 and April 16, 1912. Availability: Scarce. Value: $125.

 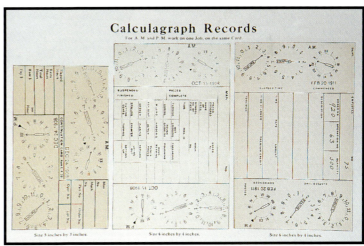

Calculagraph. Manufactured by the Calculagraph Company of 50 Church Street, New York, New York. It may be a stretch to call this a calculator as it was more like an elapsed time recorder. It computed and printed the elapsed time between the start and finish of a project. It was one of those special application calculators that created a particular marketing niche and proved to be quite successful. (c.1928) Availability: Common. Value: $150.

46 Calculagraph

Two offices using the Calculagraph for different applications.

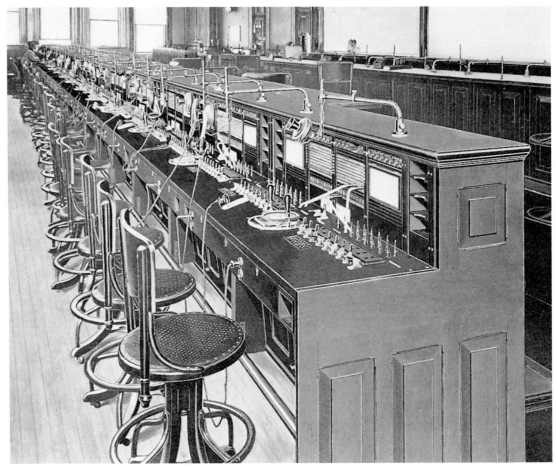

Calcumeter 47

Calculator (A). Manufactured by the Calculator Corporation of Grand Rapids, Michigan. It was one of a variety of small, inexpensive, stylus-operated, handheld, cogged disk adding machines that surfaced around 1908. Other similar machines were the Lightning; the Pangborn; the Figurator or the Ray; and the Calcumeter. This particular model did not have result windows at the top of the disks. Availability: Common. Value: $25.

Calculator (B). A stylus-operated vertical cogged slide bar capable of addition and subtraction. Made in Japan. Availability: Common. Value: $5.

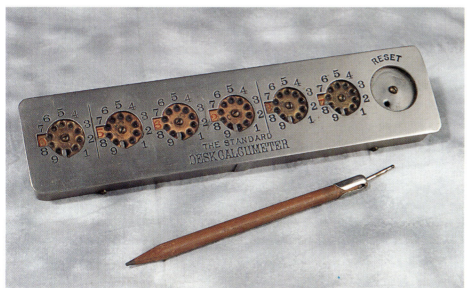

Left and below:
Calcumeter. A very well-manufactured variety of the circular cogged wheel devices. Pictured are both the 6 and 7 column units. Both come with reset mechanisms. Availability: Common. Value: $200.

48 Cardboard

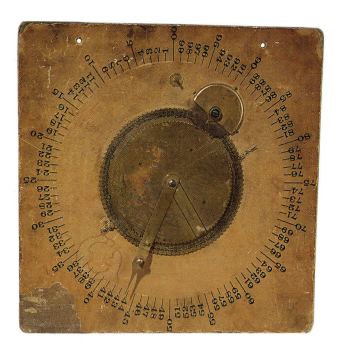

Chadwick. Small plastic adding machine made in Japan under different names. Availability: Common. Value: $15.

Cardboard Adder (A). A single mechanism unit resembling the Webb-type figure-eight adder. The author is unaware of the name of the manufacturer of this adder. Availability: Rare. Value: $700.

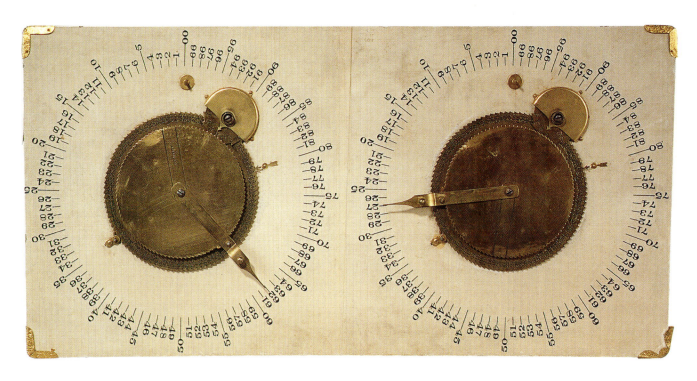

Cardboard Adder (B). A double mechanism unit that is identical to the single mechanism one. It does not carry over to the second unit automatically. Availability: Rare. Value: $1,200.

Clary

The Clary Adding Machine Company of Searcy, Arkansas produced both a ten- and full-keyboard configuration machine during the late 1950s. It was a well-designed adding machine with fewer working parts then most on the market at the time. The Clary factory in Searcy was considered an extremely modern manufacturing facility. Remington Rand purchased the company and factory in the early 1960s.

Left and above:
Clary (Model 188). Manufactured by the Clary Multiplier Corporation of Los Angeles, California. A full-keyboard, listing, electric adding machine. Serial number: 79,090. Availability: Common. Value: $35.

Clary (Model 120). Full-keyboard, hand-operated, listing adding machine. Serial number: 716,565. Availability: Common. Value: $25.

Clary (Model 168). Electric, 10-key keyboard with serial number 755,633. Availability: Common. Value: $35.

Commonwealth. Manufactured by the Commonwealth Adding Machine Company of Muskegon, Michigan and invented by George Browning. Not only is this a very rare machine, it is a very unusual one. It is a ten key, seven column, non-printing adding machine. There are two rows of windows positioned above the keyboard. One row checked the operator's entries and the top row is the result register. It is reported that a printing machine was also made. Only two are known to exist by the author. (c.1915) Availability: Rare. Value: $3,500+.

Comptometer - *see Felt and Tarrant*

Left and above:
Computator (Model 509F). Manufactured by London Computator Limited, 39 St. James Street, London, S. W. 1. Serial number: 54,587. Availability: Scarce. Value: $75.

Consul. Known as "The Educated Monkey." It is a very unique mechanical calculator. By the clever use of the monkey's arms and feet, one can perform arithmetic functions. For instance, when moving the feet to point to two different numbers, the arms point to the product (answer). (c.1920) Availability: Scarce. Value: $175.

Contex. Manufactured by CMI, Inc. Serial number: 67,332. (c.1955) Availability: Common. Value: $25.

Conto (Models A and C). Manufactured by Carl Landolt, Thalwil, Switzerland. A well-made, small adding machine with six, eight, ten or eleven columns which were circles of numbers from 1 to 0. The Conto has two rows of display windows. One row located at the top of the machine and one row at the bottom. A clock-like pointer is in the center of each column. To operate, one must move the pointer to the desired number and then activate a thumb lever located above the face plate. The number then appears in the top display window. (c.1912) Availability: Rare. Value, each: $1,000.

52 Corexa

Corexa. Manufactured by Cirena S. A., of Geneva, Switzerland and distributed by the Hilner International Corporation of Los Angeles, California. Serial number: 24,718. It was capable of addition, subtraction, and multiplication with portability the major feature. Availability: Scarce. Value: $50.

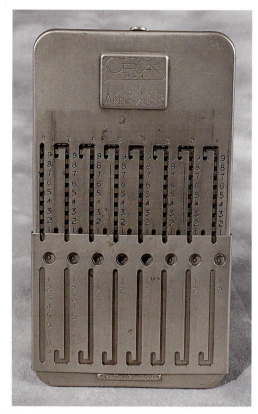

Cray Pocket Arithmometer. Manufactured by the Cray Arithmometer Company of Ithaca, New York. A stylus-operated vertical slide bar adder capable of addition and subtraction. Availability: Common. Value: $25.

Corona Adding Machine. Manufactured by the Portable Adding Machine Company of Syracuse, New York. The serial number of the above machine is AIP0236. It was a full-keyboard printer. Availability: Common. Value: $25.

Curta Calculator (Model 1). Manufactured by Contina, LTD / Vaduz, Liechtenstein. While the Curta Calculator is small in size for a mechanical calculator, it is big in features. It not only solves four rule problems but also can extract square roots, figure percentages, has accumulative multiplication, multiplication or division by constant factor, percentage of increase or decrease, compound percentages, distance and azimuth-linear, and interpolation (solves formulae). All of the control mechanisms are pictured and identified in the pictures below. There were two models of the Curta. The Model 1, which has a diameter of 2.0625" and a capacity of 8 x 6 x 11. The Model 2, which has a diameter of 2.5625" and a capacity of 11 x 8 x 15. Serial number: 55, 726. (c.1948) Availability (each): Scarce. Value (each): $600.

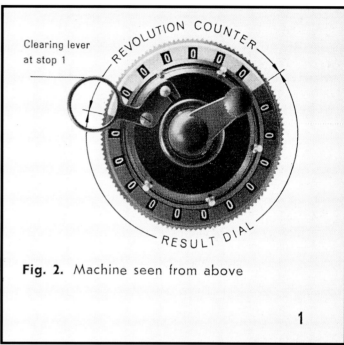

Fig. 2. Machine seen from above

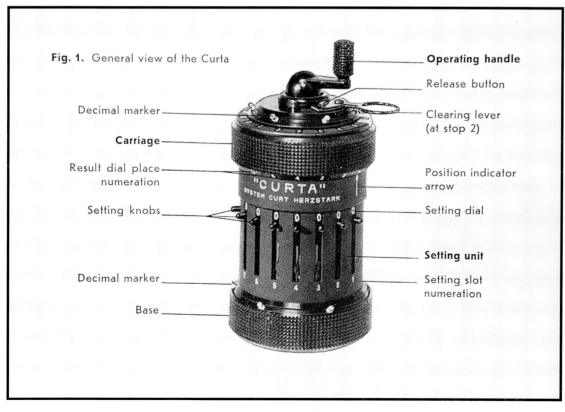

54 Dactyle

Dactyle. A pinwheel calculator based on Odhner patents. It originally appeared under the name of Chateau in 1905 and was manufactured in Paris, France. Availability: Scarce. Value: $400.

Below left and below right:
Dalton (Glass Side Model 1). One of the most popular American adding machines of all time. Invented by Hubert Hopkins, the same person who designed the Moon-Hopkins typewriter/adding machine. The popularity of the Dalton was probably attributable to its ten-key keyboard. It allowed operators to use a faster touch method for inputting figures. The early model of the Dalton and the most collectible has beveled glass on both sides and in front of the machine. (c.1902) Availability (Model 1): Scarce. Value: $450. Availability (all other models): Common. Value (all other models): $50.

Dial-A-Matic 55

Darnley's Patent. A school children's pencil holder that also served as a multiplier. By holding the device with both hands and lining up the left-hand numbers to be multiplied and then by following the equal sign and line across to a window, you found the answer displayed. It was also called Darnley's Patent Rotatable Lightning Calculator, Pencil Case, Ruler & Measurer. Manufactured by the Solely Manufacturing Company in England. The British patent number was 167,699/21. The German patent number was 797,458. Availability: Scarce. Value: $25.

Right:
Denominator (A). Manufactured by the Denominator Adding Machine Company of Brooklyn, New York. A special application machine designed to tally the number of different coins needed for payroll. It was not an adding machine. (c.1915) Availability: Common. Value: $125.

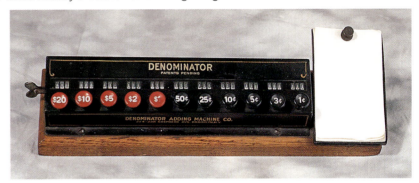

Denominator (B). Manufactured by the Denominator Adding Machine Co., New York. There are two United States patents listed on the machine: 2,572,784 and 2,726,040. It is a 12 column machine that is 16.75" long x 2" wide. Serial number: 138,514. Availability: Scarce. Value: $50.

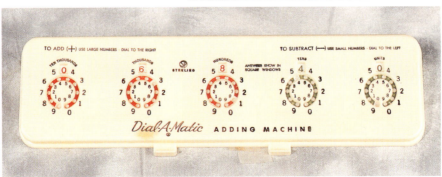

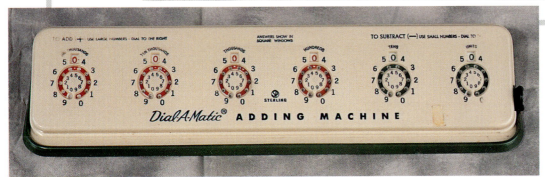

Dial-A-Matic. Four-, five-, and six-column machines, plastic, cogged wheel inexpensive adders. Availability: Common. Value (each): $15.

Dollad. A cardboard stylus-type adder manufactured by the ADEM Company of Philadelphia, Pennsylvania. Availability: Common. Value: $10.

Ellis. *See Chapter Four: Combination Adding Machines and Typewriters.*

A Calculating Machine which Electrically Adds, Multiplies, Divides and Subtracts.

The Ensign

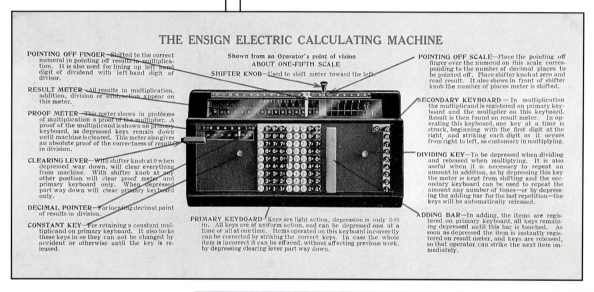

Ensign. Manufactured by the Ensign Company of Boston, Massachusetts, at their 385-387 Broadway, New York City, New York, facility. The Ensign is an electric, full-keyboard calculator with direct subtraction and division. It was available in three different models: the Model 97 (9 x 7 x 16); Model 75 (7 x 5 x 12; and Model 54 (5 x 4 x 9). The machine pictured above is a Model 54 with serial number 220. It has a patent date of November 1, 1904 held by Emory A. Ensign of Boston, Massachusetts, and a patent number of 773,632. It weighs 50 pounds. Availability: Rare. Value: $1,000.

Facit 57

Everest. A ten-key keyboard hand-operated adding machine. Serial number: 211,834. It was made in Italy. Availability: Common. Value: $35.

Facit (Model ESA-0). Manufactured by Atuidaberg-Facit Company of Sweden. Serial number: 347,341. Availability: Common. Value: $50.

Facit (Model Cal-13). Manufactured by Atuidaberg-Facit Company of Sweden. Serial number: 633,160. Availability: Common. Value: $50.

Federal

Federal. This full-keyboard adding machine was manufactured by the Colt's Patent Fire Arms Manufacturing Company of Hartford, Connecticut. However, it was owned and marketed by the Federal Adding Machine Co., Inc. of New York, New York. This machine originally appeared under the name of the White Adding Machine. (c.1913) Availability: Scarce. Value: $250.

Federal Adding Machine Company founder, Charles Wales. The famous gun manufacturer, Colt's Patent Fire Arms Manufacturing Company of Hartford, Connecticut, manufactured the machine for Federal.

of the United States; an analysis of every detail that offered possibility of improvement.

Certainty of Uninterrupted Satisfaction

TODAY we know, what was not realized in 1900 or in 1890, when the design that is still adhered to by older machines was adopted—An adding machine is a *service-purchase*. The mechanism is one fourth of it. Three fourths of it is your confident knowledge that the responsibility of the maker follows the machine, to ensure your uninterrupted satisfaction in its use. You are buying its work, and the certainty that it will work whenever you want it to.

Designed for Modern Service Requirements

UNINTERRUPTED satisfaction depends not merely on the good intentions of the maker, nor on constant adjustments by inspectors; fundamentally it depends on the design of the machine—and responsibilities have now tied their makers. The Federal-A is *designed* for service that will ensure your continuous satisfaction. Years after you purchase it we can fulfill our responsibilities, not only with greater speed and satisfaction to you, but at far less cost to ourselves. That fact also reduces greatly the cost-per-year of using a Federal.

74 Years Ahead; and 150 Percent Better

EVERY adding machine user knows all the details of general efficiency and value in an adding machine. Experts, by comparisons with the best other machines in the market, have made an estimate of the increased value in the Federal-A. It represents about two and a half times the value of any machine of similar capabilities and price. It is the highest product of *modern* engineering knowledge and processes, which in 1919 bear in mind, are 50 years ahead of 1914, and 74 years ahead of the year 1890.
—*Charles Wales.*

EVERY Federal-A Adding Machine bears the name of Colt's Patent Fire Arms Manufacturing Company, who produce it under patents and designs owned by the Federal Adding Machine Corporation. Realize the significance of that. Do not confuse it with ordinary orders for "parts." Hundreds of firms would be willing to make parts. Colt's will not make anything for which they are not willing to take full responsibility. They have never made anything that was "Second best." Their name on the Federal Machine is a declaration not only of responsibility, but of pride in the product.

Colt's Own Tests Guard the Colt Reputation

IN addition to our own inspection and test of each Federal machine, Colt's themselves, before delivery, make their own rigorous tests, proving for themselves that every machine is perfect, and is truly representative of the quality and efficiency that have always characterized every Colt's product. Nearly every Government in the world buys from Colt's. The reputation of Colt's has been increasing for over 75 years; it is worth millions of dollars. They could not afford to put their name on a single article which might injure that reputation.

Facilities Which Produced the Browning Gun

THE Browning Machine Gun, one of the greatest metallurgical and precision achievements in the War, was perfected and made in Colt's plant at Hartford. Every detail of new knowledge, new processes, and new production equipment, gained at the cost of millions, was concentrated on that task. They have now been applied to the production of the Federal-A. Anyone who knows the Browning Gun knows that it has a toughness of metal, and a durability, infinitely greater than were possible five years ago.

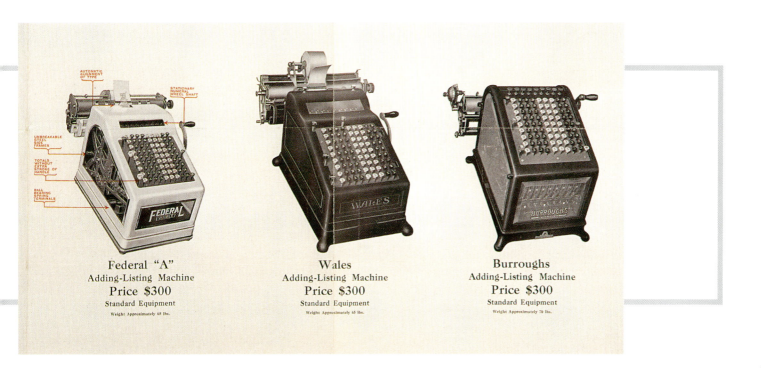

Feliks. A Russian calculator based on the pinwheel principle of Odhner. (c.1935) Availability: Scarce. Value: $375.

Felt & Tarrant

Dorr E. Felt, a young mechanic in Chicago, Illinois, began working on a calculator that would eliminate the ever-present hand crank on the right side of the machine. Using the hand crank was time consuming and labor intensive. To activate the mechanism the operator first had to depress the keys desired, then remove his hands from the key tops, and finally pull the hand crank forward for each amount. Felt's idea was to develop a "live keyboard" and do away with the need for a hand crank. Not having access to expensive machining tools Felt improvised. In the year 1885 he went to a grocery shop and procured a wooden macaroni box. To this he added some skewers, rubber bands and staples to build his now famous *macaroni box model*. His first machines were placed on the market in 1887. That same year he started the Felt & Tarrant Manufacturing Company in Chicago, Illinois. The identity of his partner, Tarrant, has been lost over the years. In any case, Felt was the dominant partner. His first machine mechanisms were metal but the frames that housed the mechanism were made of wood. Machines with serial numbers below 15,000 have wooden cases and they are considered the most collectible.

Dorr E. Felt, inventor of the Felt & Tarrant

Macaroni Box Advertising

Felt and Tarrant Plant in Chicago, Illinois

Felt & Tarrant 61

First Model with wooden case. Serial number: 408. (c.1887) Availability: Rare. Value: $3,000.

Below:
Comptograph. Felt's first printer model. It also had a wood case. The patent number was 341,973. (c.1889) This was the first printing adding machine to appear on the market. The above example is the only machine the author knows to exist in a private collection. Availability: Rare. Value: $8,000

62 Felt & Tarrant

Comptometer (Model A). Serial number: 19,827. (c.1903) Availability: Scarce. Value: $800.

Above and left:
Comptometer (Model J). The serial number of pictured machine is 285,352. (c.1928) Availability: Common. Value: $35.

Felt & Tarrant 63

Comptometer (Model JS). The serial number of pictured machine is 335,117. Availability: Scarce. Value: $800.

Above and right:
Comptometer (Model E with Control Key). A brochure and a picture of an early training class. Availability: Common. Value: $75.

64 Felt & Tarrant

Comptometer (Model K). The serial number of pictured machine is K868,329. Availability: Common. Value: $50.

Below and right:
Comptometer (Model M). The serial number of pictured machine is M487,605. Availability: Common. Value: $50.

Fites-Peerless. Manufactured by Less T. Fite in Murfreeboro, Tennessee. This special application calculator was designed for the egg farmers to determine the price of eggs when sold in either dozens or odd number lots. Availability: Scarce. Value: $50.

Fowler. Manufactured by the Fowler Adding Machine Company at 212 Broadway, Corner of Fulton Street in New York, New York. Patented by George B. Fowler on July 14, 1869. Also marketed under the name Universal. A slide bar-type adder with a knob on left to lock bars in place. Availability: Rare. Value: $1,000.

66 Friden

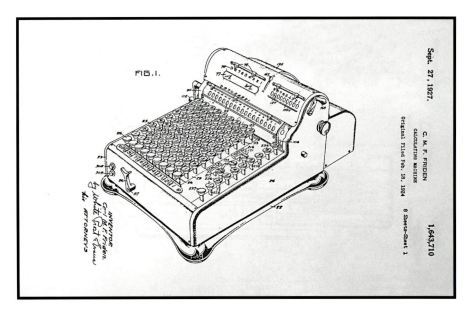

Friden (Model ST-10). One of the rotary varieties of calculators. Instead of printing on paper, it registered the numbers on dials and was much faster than a printing calculator. These dials were located on a moving carriage on top of the unit. The Friden also had a ten-key keyboard located at the lower left-hand side of the regular keyboard. It was used for automatic multiplication and division. Serial number: 173,151. Availability: Common. Value: $150.

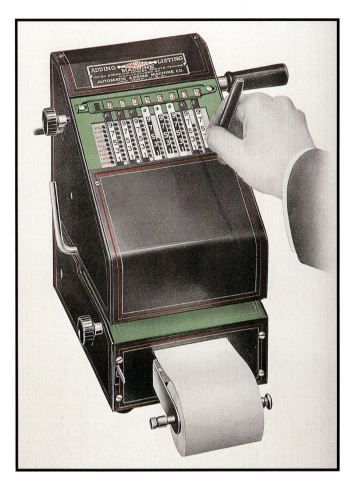

Gancher. *See Golden Gem.* Both machines were the same and manufactured by the Automatic Adding Machine Company of New York, New York. This particular model was a printing version and appeared about 1915. Availability: Rare. Value: $1,000.

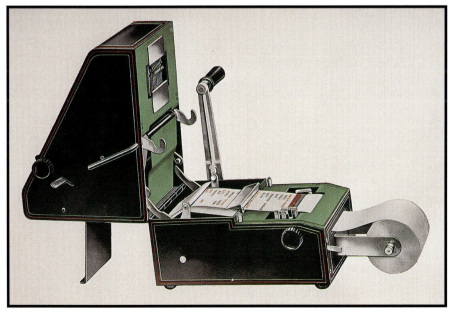

Golden Gem

The brainchild of Abraham J. Gancher and manufactured by the Automatic Adding Machine Company of New York, New York, this little adder can be found almost everywhere antiques are sold. That alone is a testimonial to its popularity and the success of the company's original sales thrust. It was introduced in 1904. There are several models in the author's collection.

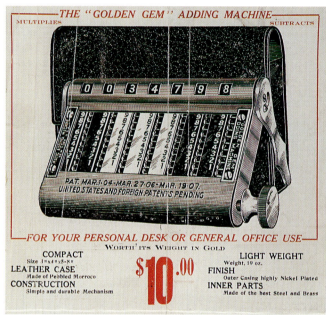

Above and right:
Golden Gem (Standard Model). Manufactured by the Automatic Adding Machine Company, New York. It was nickel-plated and includes the original case and instructions. Dimensions: 4.125" x 3.250". Serial number: 403,848. Availability: Common. Value: $75.

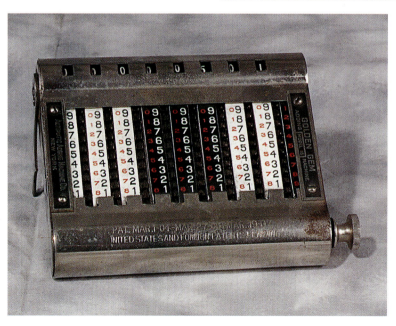

Golden Gem (Model 16). Manufactured by the Automatic Adding Machine Company, New York. This was larger than the standard model and is a little more difficult to find. Dimensions: 4.875" x 4.250". Serial number: 95,006. Availability: Scarce. Value: $125.

Golden Gem (Black Case Model). Manufactured by the Automatic Adding Machine Company, New York. Serial number: 406,889. Availability: Common. Value: $75.

Right:
Golden Gem (with nickel-plated metal stand). Manufactured by the Automatic Adding Machine Company, New York. The United Stated patent dates are March 4, 1904 and March 27, 1906. Serial number: 15,590. Availability: Scarce. Value: $250.

Golden Gem (The Improved Gem). Manufactured by the Automatic Adding Machine Company, New York. This model is housed in an attractive oak case. United States patent dates are March 1, 1904; March 27, 1906; March 19, 1907. Serial number: 30,411. Also pictured is the operator's guide. Availability: Rare. Value: $500.

Groesbeck. Manufactured by Ziegler and McCudry and was distributed by C. H. Crittenden of Philadelphia, Pennsylvania. The United States patent date is March 1, 1870. Availability: Rare. Value: $3,000.

Hamann-Manus. Manufactured by the Deutsche Telephonwerke und Kabelindustrie Aktiengesellschaft, Berlin, Germany. The machine looks very similar to the pinwheel Odhner or Baldwin type, but employed a new mechanical principle, called a "geared wheel". (c.1925) Availability: Scarce. Value: $400.

Hart. The inventor of this small circular adder was William Hart of Kirksville, Missouri. It was patented on January 15, 1878 and issued patent number 199,289. Availability: Rare. Value: $4,500.

Hasbro. A plastic toy adder manufactured by the Hasbro Company. It had plastic gears as well. It was a 5-column adder with a total and clear key. Availability: Common. Value: $15.

Herring, J. L. Designed by J. L. Herring of Derry, Pennsylvania. This adder very much resembled the Webb Adder of 1868; however, it was specifically designed for computing railroad tonnage resistance. (c.1925) Availability: Scarce. Value: $500.

Hatfield. Invented and manufactured by A. L. Hatfield of Lewisburg, Pennsylvania in 1854. Patent Number: 11,726. Patent date: September 26, 1854. The serial number of this particular specimen is 354. This early American adder consists of three circular brass wheels, calibrated and rotatable. An indicator is mounted on top of these three wheels and when positioned properly, shows the result in a small rectangular cutout. The Hatfield is the first of this type of adder known to the author. Later variations of this type of adder were the Hart, the Webb, and the L.C. Smith. Availability: Rare. Value: $5,000.

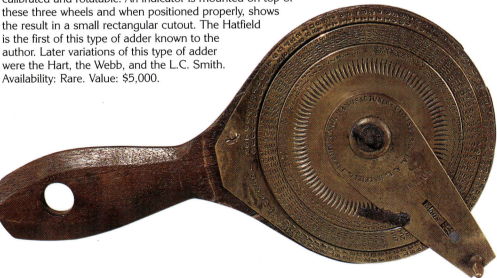

Herring, J. L.

Herring, J. L. Keuffel & Esser model. Availability: Scarce. Value: $500.

Below:
Hoffritz. Manufactured in West Germany. A finger ratchet-type of adding machine with the result appearing in small windows above the keyboard. Availability: Common, Value: $25.

Below:
Hines Patent Calculator. An English device that calculated pounds and ounces. It was manufactured by Hines Patents, Ltd., of Glasgow, Scotland. Dimensions: 5.25" w x 4.75" h x 22.5" long. Availability: Rare. Value: $2,000.

Högfors. A small Swedish adding machine in which the operator placed her finger between two teeth opposite the number that was to be added and pulled down until the finger stopped against the cover. The handle at left of machine reset to "0." Totals are visible in little windows in line with the word "Total." Serial number: 47,558. Availability: Common. Value: $50.

Itemizer. A product of Clemans-Joyce, Merchandise Mart, Chicago, 54, Illinois. An adding and subtracting device designed for women shoppers, to be worn on three fingers of their hand. Availability: Common. Value: $15.

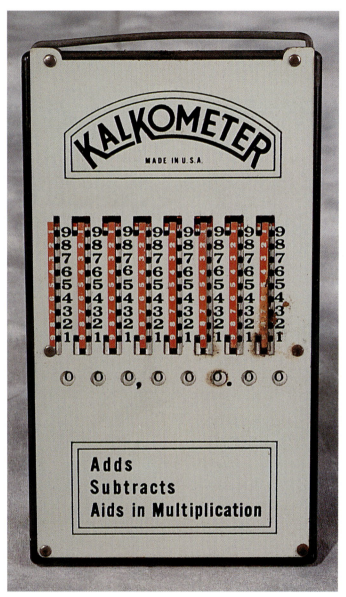

Kalkometer. Stylus-operated vertical cogged slide bar with addition and subtraction. Availability: Common. Value: $5.

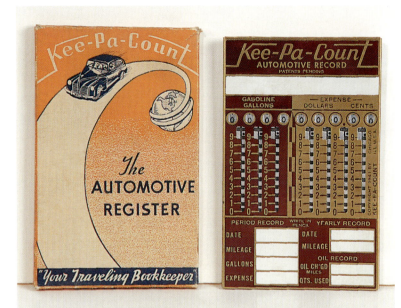

Kee-Pa-Count. An automotive register traveling bookkeeper that kept track of miles per gallon and expenses. Manufactured by the Kee-Pa-Count Company of Chicago, Illinois. Availability: Common. Value: $35.

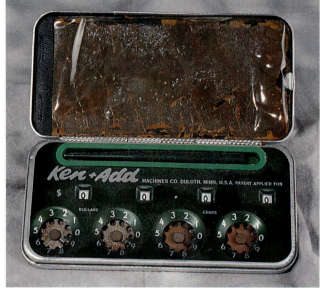

Ken + Add. A small four-column adder that used Pascal-type cogged wheels. It was manufactured by the Ken + Add Machines Company of Duluth, Minnesota. It weighed only 5.7 ounces. Availability: Common. Value: $5.

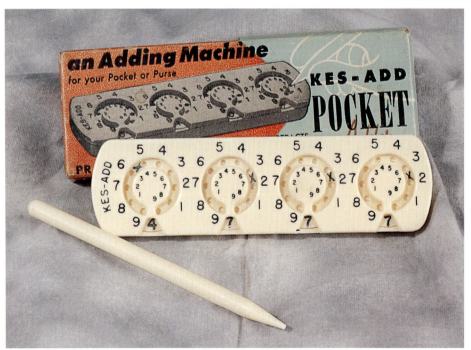

Kes-Add. A pocket adder manufactured by the Kesling Pocket Adder Company of St. Louis, Missouri and distributed by the Hart Vance Company, also of St. Louis, Missouri. This four column plastic adder weighed only 1.2 ounces. Patent Number: 2,450,468. (c.1948) Availability: Common. Value: $10.

Key Adding Machine. Manufactured by the Key Adding & Subtracting Machine Company at 942 Sante Street in Los Angeles, California. The inventor was J. F. Key. This American adder consists of two cylindrical wheels that are rotated by the use of a stylus. The right-hand wheel added in units of 10 to 99 and the left-hand wheel added in units of 100. Serial number: 480. Dimensions: 4.5" h. x 13.5" long. Availability: Rare. Value: $3,000.

Lamb Calculator (Model A). Manufactured by the Calculator Manufacturing Company, Inc., of New York, New York. Patented on May 27, 1913. This was a payroll calculator and computed hourly wages, hours worked, etc. Availability: Scarce. Value: $300.

Leavitt Calculator. A very early American calculator that was designed to compute interest. A United States patent was issued to William B. Leavitt of New Hampshire in 1845. Dimensions: 12.25" diameter. Stereotyped by Morill Silsby & Company. Availability: Rare. Value: $800.

Lightning

Above two photos:
Lightning. Manufactured by the Calculator Company of Grand Rapids, Michigan in 1908. The Lightning with its many variations is the most common machine a collector will find. They are everywhere. It is operated by the use of a stylus and features a tens-carry mechanism. Availability: Common. Value: $25.

Lightning (Cardboard Version). This cardboard version of the Lightning Adding Machine resembles the Webb adder. It is a stylus-operated adder with the results shown at the top in both units and hundreds. Instructions are printed on the reverse side. The manufacturer and date it first appeared are unknown to the author. Availability: Rare. Value: $600.

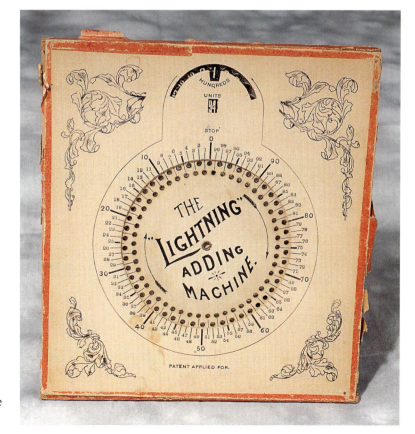

78 Lightning

Lightning (Figure-eight – Webb Type).
Also see Webb Adding Machine

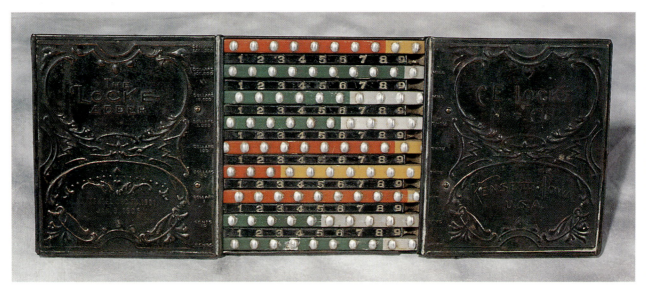

Locke Adder. Invented and patented by C. E. Locke of Wisconsin in December, 1901. Patent Number: 689,680. This was a sliding bar-type adder with color-coding to readily tell dollars and cents. There were two models of the Locke adder; one dated 1901 and a second model dated 1905. Availability: Scarce. Value (each): $800.

MADAS. Manufactured by H. W. Egli, A. G. of Zurich, 2 Switzerland. Erwin Jahnz saw a need for a stepped drum-type calculator that had automatic division and invented the MADAS in 1908. The name Madas is an acronym for: "**M**ultiplication, **A**ddition, **D**ivision **A**nd **S**ubtraction." United States patent dated: December 10, 1913. Serial number: 5,341. Availability: Rare. Value: $2,500.

Marbel's Blood Cell Calculator (Model V1-T). Manufactured by Dr. M. M. Marbel of the Marbel Blood Calculator Company, at 3267 South Halstead Street, of Chicago, Illinois. According to the manufacturer, the machine was capable of "Percentage calculation for differential blood films and an adding machine for Erythrocytes, Lencocytes, and blood platelets." Patented: June 6, 1922. Availability: Common. Value: $35.

Below and below left:
Marchant. Manufactured by the Marchant Calculating Machine Company of Oakland, California. First appeared as a pinwheel-type machine in 1911. Initially, there were two models, the Pony and the Standard. They differed only in size and capacity. Marchant merged with the Smith Corona Typewriter Company in the 1950s, and became known as Smith Corona Marchant or SCM.

Magic Multiplying Pencil. Manufactured and patented by the Apex Products Corp., of New York. This was probably designed for the educational market. It is a wood pencil with which simple multiplication can be performed by twisting the top of the pencil until the numbers you wish to multiply are lined up at the very top of the pencil. The result appears directly under this action, enclosed in a window. Dimensions: .50" diameter x 6" long. Availability: Common. Value: $10.

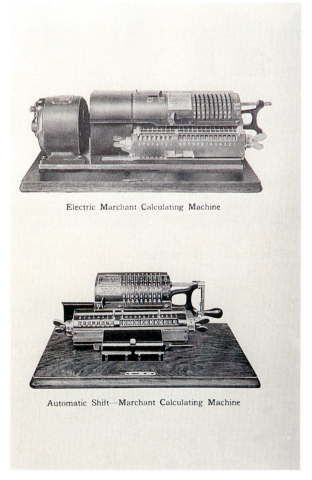

Marchant (Standard Model A). The capacity of this model was 9 x 8 x 13. It had a wood base and the pictured machine has the very low serial number of 941. Availability: Common. Value: $175.

Marchant (Standard Model B). This was the higher capacity version of the Standard. It had a wood base and column capacity of 9 x 10 x 18. Serial number: 75,273. Patent date: February 22, 1916. Availability: Common. Value: $175.

Marchant (Model XLA). An example of a compact, lever-set, 9 x 8 x 13 capacity pinwheel Marchant. Serial number: XLA 1,147. Availability: Common. Value: $175.

Marchant (Model XL). Larger pinwheel machine that shows a patent date of February 22, 1916. Serial number: XL96,255. Availability: Scarce. Value: $200.

Marchant (Model KC). This was the first keyboard model Marchant. The KC model has a capacity of 9 x 9 x 18. There also was a Model KA (6 x 6 x 12) and a Model KB (9 x 8 x 16) places. Serial number: 5,254. Availability: Scarce. Value: $250.

Marchant (Model H910114). This was the 1923 keyboard model. It was the first keyboard electric model with an outboard motor. Serial number: 10,065. Availability: Scarce. Value: $250.

Marchant (Model ACR8D). A rotary-type model. Serial number: 162,304. Availability: Common. Value: $75.

Master Adding Machine. A Belgium adder whose action resembled the stylus-operated Addiator. (c.1935) Availability: Common. Value: $75.

Mechanical Accountant. Manufactured by the Mechanical Accounting Company of Providence, Rhode Island, and designed by J. A. V. Turck. This key-driven adding and calculating machine appeared on the market in 1900 and was sold through direct mail. With the first simplex models, you were limited to adding in only one column at a time, but later duplex models had the ability to add in more than one column at a time. Availability: Scarce. Value: $300.

Meilicke Calculator

Meilicke Calculator. Manufactured by the Meilicke Calculating Systems, Inc. of Chicago, Illinois. This company created its own marketing niche by compiling lists of tables that could be used for various mathematical applications. Their earlier products consisted of books and cards arranged as in a vertical file. A later model, such as the pictured specimen, was designed for commercial banking interest computed at various rates. (c. 1930) Availability: Scarce. Value: $125.

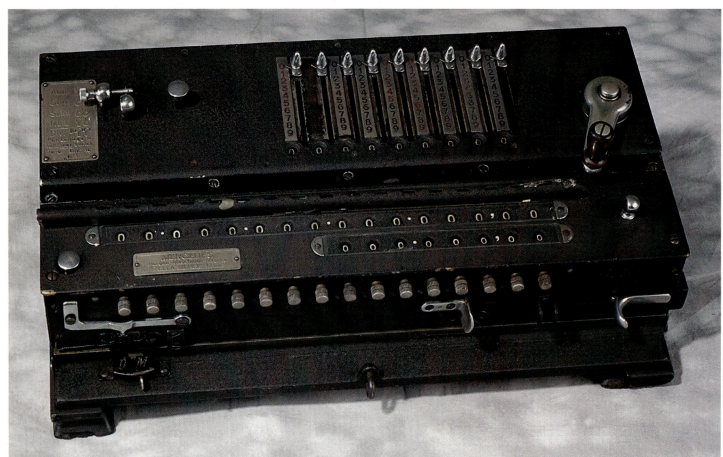

Mercedes-Euklid. Manufactured by the Mercedes Office Machine Works, Charlottenburg, Berlin, Germany. This was the first calculator model to contain a new mechanical system. It was a manual lever-set calculator with automatic division. The inventor was Christian Hamann. (c. 1905) Availability: Rare. Value: $2,000.

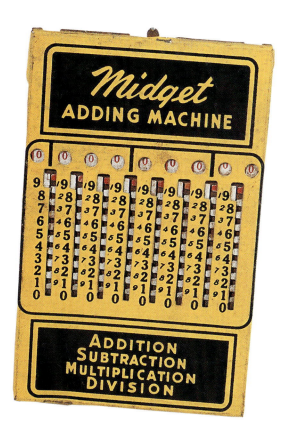

Midget. A stylus-type adder capable of four functions with yellow gold finish. Availability: Common. Value: $15.

Midget. Manufactured by the Midget Machine Company of Brooklyn, New York. This was probably one of the most unique little adders of its time. The Midget was a hand-held adder that was originally introduced in 1910 and sold for only $10. It is very well made and highly prized among collectors. Serial number: 1,118. Availability: Rare. Value: $5,000.

Millionaire

Invented by Otto Steiger in 1893 and manufactured by Hans W. Egli of Zurich, Switzerland. Originally introduced as a manual lever-set flatbed-type arithmometer. Later keytops were added and it was electrically operated.

Advertisement of the front of the Millionaire.

Advertisement showing the inside of the Millionaire.

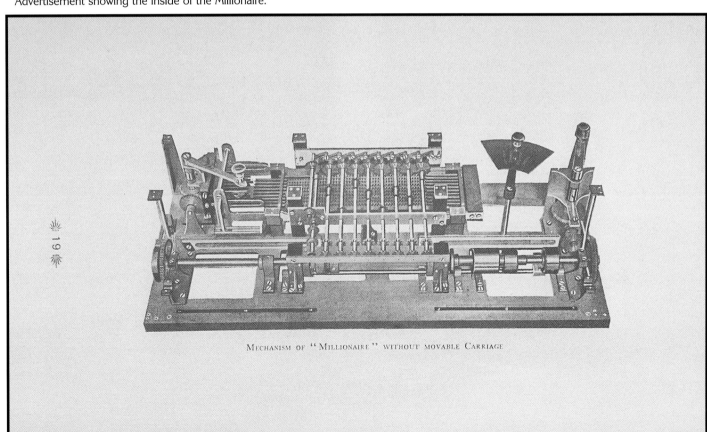

Millionaire (Lever-set Model). The pictured machine has a serial number of 1,775. Availability: Rare. Value: $2,500.

Millionaire (Electric Key Top Model). The pictured machine has a serial number of 2,893. Availability: Rare. Value: $2,000.

Monroe

In 1872, Frank Stephen Baldwin, the inventor of the pinwheel mechanism and the Baldwin calculator, teamed with James R. Monroe to develop another calculator with a different mechanical principle (the variable tooth gear). It was to become the first Monroe calculator. Working at Blair's Tool Shop at the corner of Greenwich and Spring Street in New York, New York, they developed a finished product. On June 15, 1912, Baldwin applied for patent number 890,888 and it was granted on June 16, 1908. A second patent, number 1,080,245, was applied for on December 2, 1913.

After the Pike Adding Machine Company, of Orange, New Jersey, was sold to the Burroughs Company in 1909, Monroe moved into the former Pike plant and began production of their calculators. Continuous expansion of the Orange facility would eventually cause Monroe to make the following boast in their advertising: *"The Largest Factory in the World Engaged Exclusively in the Production of Calculating Machines."*

James R. Monroe

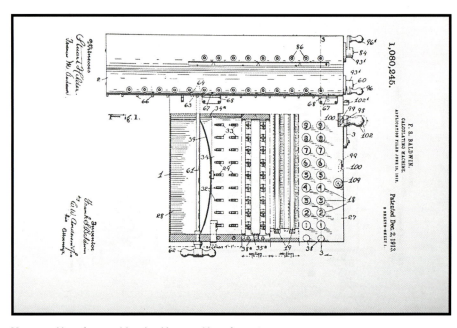

Monroe. Manufactured by the Monroe Manufacturing Company, Inc., of Orange, New Jersey.

Monroe Calculator (Model D). An early model Monroe rotary. Serial number: 2,217. Availability: Common. Value: $100.

Monroe Calculator

Above and right:
Monroe Calculator (Model KA160). This was Monroe's second electric machine. Like its predecessor, it had an outboard motor. Serial number: 55,241. Availability: Scarce. Value: $150.

Monroe Calculator (Model 209-11-042). This was the former Gardner adding machine that first appeared on the market in 1925 and was acquired by Monroe. It was a Duplex machine with two separate counters. Serial number: 16,755. Availability: Scarce. Value: $200.

Monroe Calculator

Monroe Calculator. A smaller and more common version of the Monroe calculator. Serial number: 2,217. Availability: Scarce. Value: $50.

Monroe Calculator (Model CSA8). A redesigned version of the Monroe calculator. (c.1950) Availability: Common. Value: $50.

Monroe Calculator (Model 210-285-212). This model was designed for posting bookkeeping forms. This was the basic Gardner adding machine acquired by Monroe. The two counting registers make this adding machine an ideal posting machine. Availability: Scarce. Value: $65.

Multi-Vider. The Ruxton Multi-Vider Pencil was a small device that multiplied and divided. It fit over the eraser section of a conventional pencil and was manufactured by the Chicago Recording Scale Company of Milwaukee, Wisconsin. Availability: Common. Value: $15.

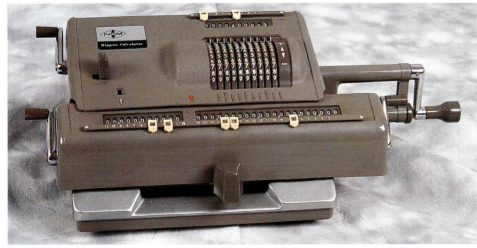

Nippon Calculator (Model HL 21). Manufactured by the Nippon Calculator Corporation of Japan. This was a 1960s version of the pinwheel action-type calculator made famous by Brunsviga, Odhner and Baldwin. Serial number: 311,049. Availability: Scarce. Value: $300.

Numeria Rotary Calculator (Model 8213). Manufactured by the Italian firm of Logomarsino of Milan, Italy. Serial number: 052,928. Availability: Common. Value: $75.

Olivetti

The Olivetti organization was established in Ivrea (Turin), Italy by Camillo Olivetti. Mr. Olivetti graduated from the University of Turin with a degree in electrical engineering. In 1893 he was asked to accompany one of his professors on a lecture tour of the universities in the United States.

As a result he was offered and accepted an "Assistant Professorship" in the Electrical Engineering Department of Stanford University in California. Olivetti remained there for one year and then return to Italy. Upon his return home, Olivetti spent several years engrossed in the study and production of electrical and mathematical devices. In 1908, he founded the Olivetti Company and concentrated completely on the production of office machines.

The first model of the Olivetti typewriter appeared in 1911. It immediately proved to be a strong competitor in the marketplace.

During the next few years, the Olivetti product line was favorably received in Italy, Belgium, Spain, Argentina, and Brazil, and the demand for them increased rapidly.

Camillo Olivetti

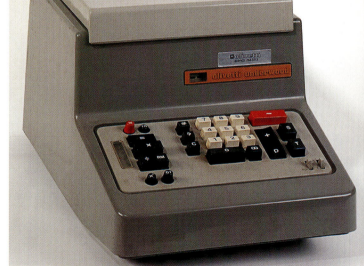

Olivetti (Model Divisumma 26 GT). Availability: Common. Value: $75.

Olivetti (Model Divisumma). Availability: Common. Value: $50.

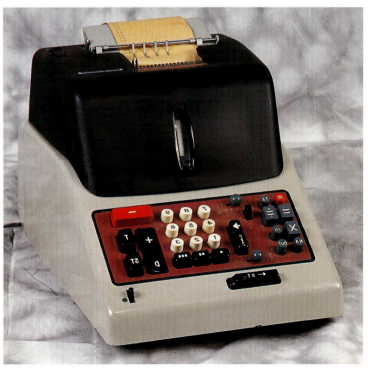

Olivetti (Model Elettro Summa 23). Availability: Common. Value: $100.

Olivetti (Model Logos 40). A calculator with styling ahead of its time by world famous industrial designer Mario Bellini. (c.1975) Availability: Common. Value: $50.

94 Original Odhner

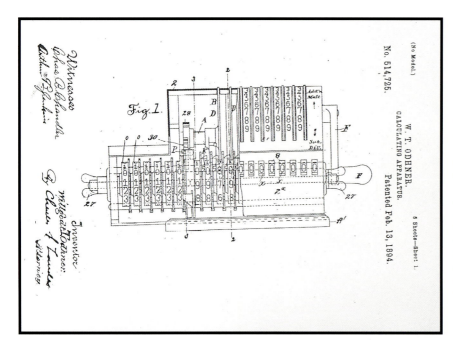

Original Odhner Patent. The 1874 invention of Willgodt T. Odhner, which employed the pinwheel system or variable tooth gear, the same principle that was patented initially by Frank S. Baldwin. A dispute as to who was the first inventor of the variable tooth gear was resolved when Baldwin proved that his invention dated back to 1872. The reason Odhner found it necessary to attach "Original" to its name was because of the existence of an identical machine manufactured by Grimme Natalis called the Brunsviga. It appears that Odhner had assigned the rights to his patent to his former employer and Natalis purchased the patent rights from his former employer. Later the Brunsviga was internationally successful; the Baldwin later became the famous Monroe Company; and the Original Odhner was later manufactured in Göteborg, Sweden by the Odhner family.

Original Odhner (Model No. 7). This calculator has ten setting levers; 13 places in the "results" display and the 8 places in the "revolution" mechanism. Serial number: 500,065. Availability: Common. Value: $125.

Original Odhner (Model No. 19). A higher capacity unit with 10 x 20 x 10. Serial number: 90,785. Availability: Common. Value: $125.

Original Odhner (Model 39). The serial number of this machine is 288,319. Availability: Common. Value: $225.

Pangborn. Manufactured by the Pangborn Calculator Company of Grand Rapids, Michigan and patented on March 5, 1907. Availability: Common. Value: $25.

96 Peerless

Above and left:
Peerless. A stepped drum-type mechanism that was manufactured in Germany beginning in 1904. The first model had a wooden case. The machine pictured was the second model with lever setting keys and a cast iron base. The advertisement is from the 1913 Kueffel & Esser catalogue. Serial number: 3,724. Availability: Rare. Value: $2,000.

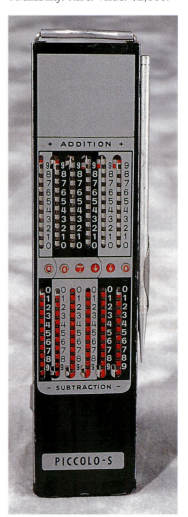

Piccolo-S. A stylus-operated vertical cogged bar adder capable of adding and subtracting. Made in Germany. Availability: Common. Value: $10.

Portable Adding Machine 97

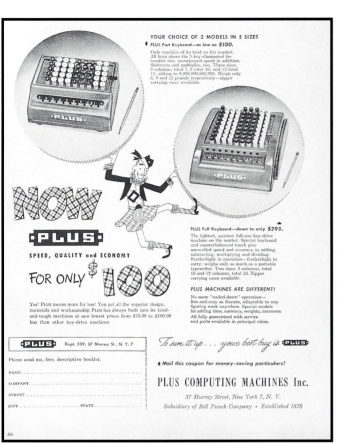

Left and below:

Plus Adding Machine. Distributed in the United States by the Plus Computing Machines, Inc., at 37 Murray Street in New York, New York. This company was a subsidiary of the Bell Punch Company of London. (c.1955) Availability: Common. Value: $35.

Portable Adding Machine. *(See Corona Adding Machine)*

Precise. A small desktop adder operated with a stylus with answers appearing on the top of the unit. To make the numbers more visible, the glass over the result was really a magnifying glass or bar. The lower front of the machine has a knob that when pulled out reveals a stylus. Patent number: 2,402,549. Made in Chicago, Illinois. Availability: Common. Value: $25.

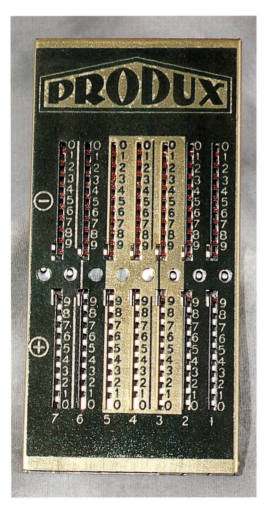

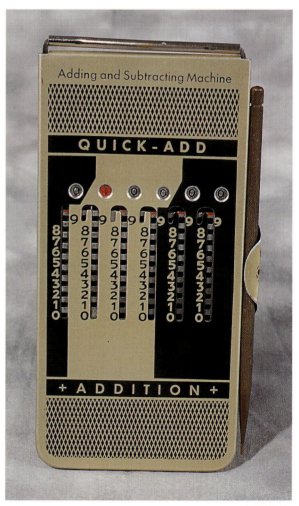

Left:
Produx. A small pocketsize adder that operated with a stylus and could add or subtract. Availability: Common. Value: $10.

Right:
Quick-Add. A stylus-operated vertical cogged slide bar adder. Addition was performed on the front of the machine and subtraction on the reverse side. It was made in Western Germany. Availability: Common. Value: $10.

Quixsum (Model C). Manufactured by the Precision Adding Machine Company, Inc. of Providence, Rhode Island, and Charlotte, North Carolina. This stylus-type adder has the ability to add hundreds, feet, inches and fractions. Patented on June 10, 1924. Serial number: 2,759. Availability: Scarce. Value: $1,800.

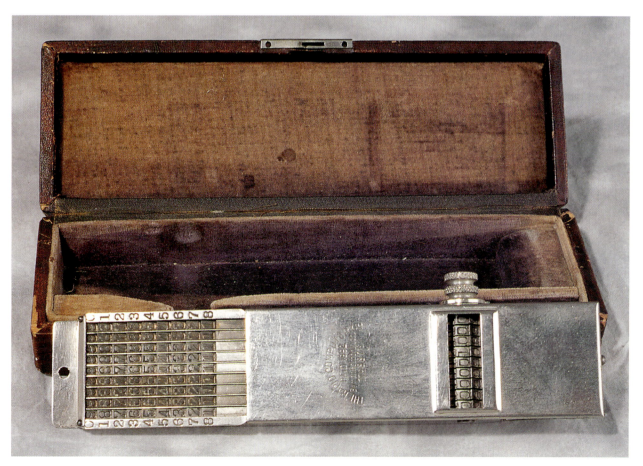

Rapid. Manufactured by the Rapid Computer Company of Benton Harbor, Michigan. (c.1893) Availability: Scarce. Value: $300.

100 Rapid

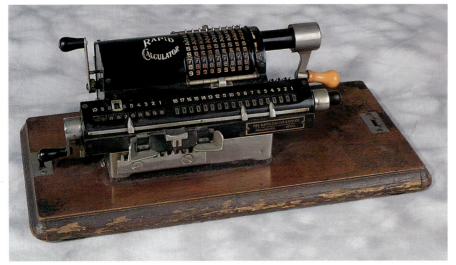

Above and right:
Rapid Calculator. Manufactured by the S. W. Allen Company at 20 South 18th Street in Philadelphia, Pennsylvania. Serial number: 6,407. (c.1923) A pinwheel-type calculator along the lines of Brunsviga, Odhner, and Baldwin. Availability: Common. Value: $250.

Rapid Adding Machine. Manufactured by the Rapid Adding Machine Company of New York. Serial number: 19,376. It was very similar to the Facit machine. Availability: Scarce. Value: $250.

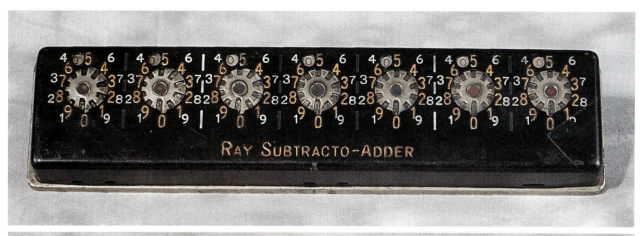

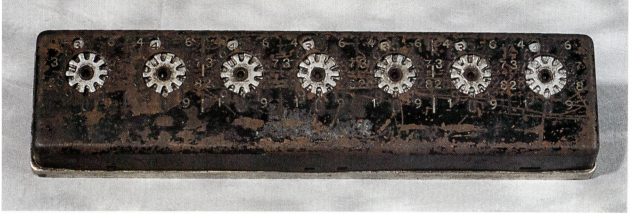

Ray. Manufactured by the Ray Adding Machine Company at 465 Washington Street in New York, New York. This was a stylus-operated device that employed a circular action similar to the Calcumeter of 1901. Serial number: 7,955. (c.1905) Availability: Scarce. Value: $175.

Reischer. A multiplier device designed for children to help them with their multiplication tables. It had a lineal keyboard with the numbers one to twelve. There are twelve windows in the top row in which the answer is displayed. The operator turned the small knob at the right of the machine until the desired number appeared. Then a key was depressed on the lower keyboard and the answer appeared in the window above. Manufactured in Argentina and protected by patent number 69,964. Availability: Scarce. Value: $25.

Remington, Remington Rand, Sperry Rand and Sperry

Portrait of James H. Rand

The Remington Rand Corporation was a conglomerate of business machine companies that were combined by the 1920s boy genius of Wall Street, James H. Rand. In 1926, Rand purchased the Remington Typewriter Company, which was owned by Wyckoff, Seamans & Benedict and made it a part of the newly formed Remington Rand Corporation.

Remington Rand Adding Machines were manufactured by Remington Rand, Inc., Accounting Machine Division of Buffalo, New York (c.1932). This was Remington Rand's first adding machine. It was also manufactured and distributed under the name Monarch. Most adding machines during this period were heavyweights. Since it weighted only 11 pounds, it is little wonder that thousands of these units were sold.

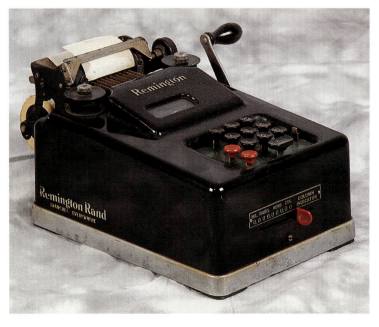

Remington Portable Adding Machine. Serial number: M20,991. Availability: Common. Value: $25.

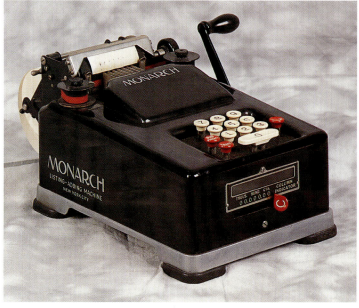

Remington (Monarch) Portable Adding Machine (Subtraction Model). Serial number: M258,930. Availability: Common. Value: $25.

Remington Adder (Model 71). A 10-key manual adder without subtraction. Serial number: 845,775. Availability: Common. Value: $25.

Left and below right:
Remington Adder (Model 73a). A 10-key manual adder without subtraction. Serial number: 556,693. Availability: Common. Value: $25.

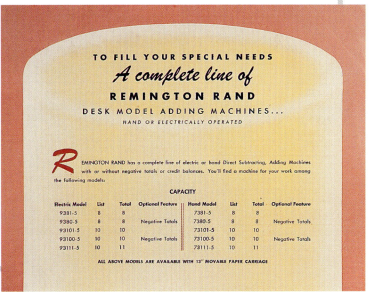

Remington Adder (New Model 73b). This was a new version of the previously mentioned Model 73a with subtraction. Serial number: 300,265. Availability: Common. Value: $75.

Remington Adder (Model 93). A 10-key electric adder with subtraction. Serial number: 135,109. Availability: Common. Value: $75.

Remington Calculator (Model 95). A 10-key electric printing calculator. Serial number: 135,109. Availability: Scarce. Value: $250.

Remington Calculator (Model 96). A 10-key electric printing calculator with lever for multiplication. To multiply, the operator had to first enter the number you wished to multiply and then hold the lever in the up position and mentally count the number of cycles heard until you reached the number by which you wished to multiply. By holding the lever in the down position you could perform short-cut multiplication. Any number over five, for instance nine would be one cycle down; eight would be two cycles down, etc. It required a special skill and sensitive touch to release the lever at just the right cycle. There were many mistakes and calculations needed to be done over again. Serial number: 456,566. Availability: Scarce. Value: $250.

Remington Calculator (Model 98). A 10-key printing electric calculator with multiplication lever and division. Serial number: 1,044,101. Availability: Common. Value: $75.

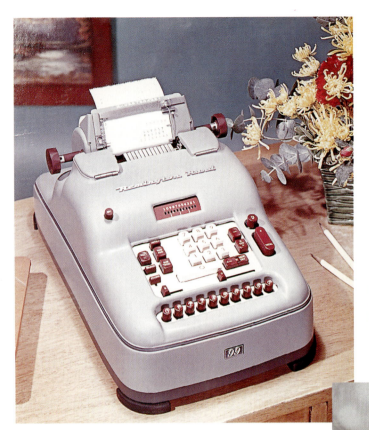

Remington Calculator (Model 99). A 10-key printing electric calculator mentioned previously in chapter on "History" to illustrate how it was demonstrated to a sales meeting. Availability: Common. Value: $75.

Remington Adding Machine (Model 102A). A Remington 10-key electric manufactured at the newly acquired Clary plant in Arkansas. Serial number: 81,062. (c.1960) Availability: Common. Value: $25.

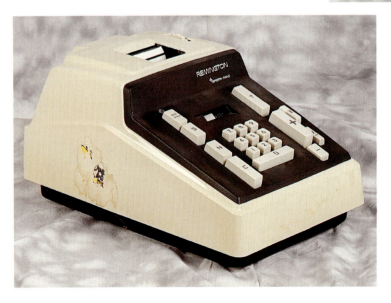

Remington Adding Machine (Model 150A). A Remington full-keyboard electric also manufactured at the Clary plant in Arkansas. Serial number: 587,740. (c.1960) Availability: Common. Value: $25.

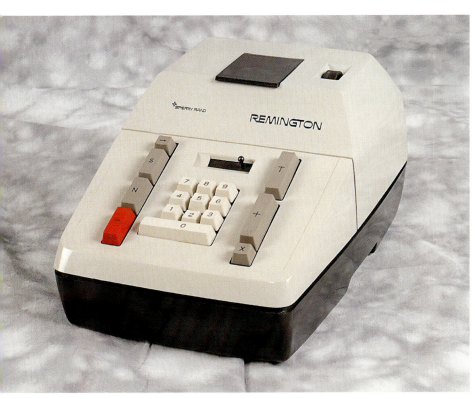

Remington Adding Machine (Model 167A).
A redesigned Remington adder manufactured from the Searcy, Arkansas plant. The internal mechanism is the same as the previous model 150A. Availability: Common. Value: $50.

Below:

Remington Adding Machine (Model 31012). This 10-key electric adding machine was probably the best adding machine ever manufactured by Remington. It had a touch that was superior to anything on the market at the time. It was manufactured at Remington's Elmira, New York, plant in the 1950s. Unfortunately, it was very expensive to build and Remington was having trouble with the union workers at the Elmira plant. To remain competitive, Remington switched production to the newly acquired Clary adding machine and manufacturing plant in Arkansas. Not only were there fewer parts in the Clary, but there was an added advantage of less labor problems in Arkansas. Serial number: 3N-1,624,192. (c.1950) Availability: Scarce. Value: $125.

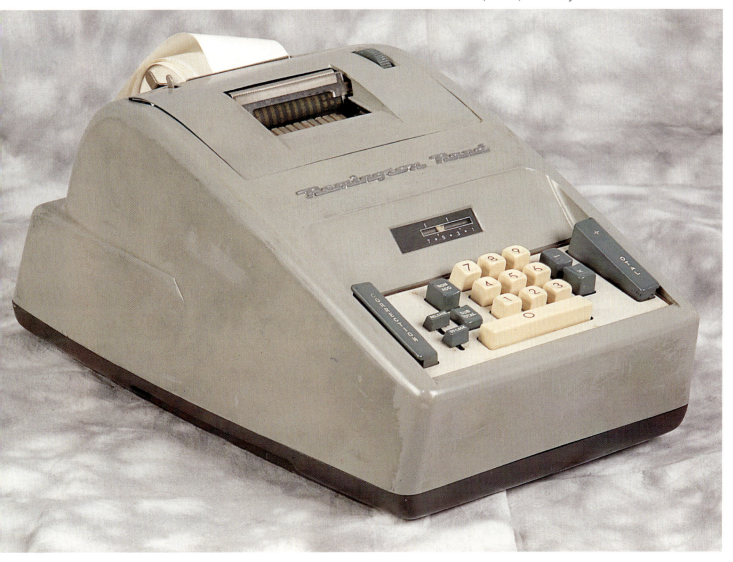

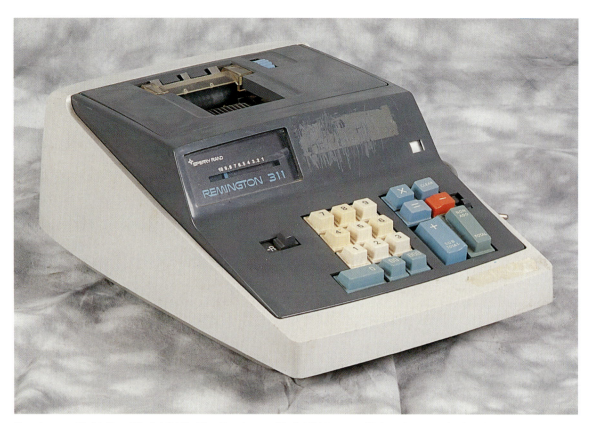

Remington Multiplier (Model 311). The Remington Model 311 was a 10-key direct multiplier that appeared in the early 1970s. It was not on the market very long as the electronic models were less expensive to build. Serial number: 61,569. Availability: Scarce. Value: $125.

Remington Rand Calculator (Model R-540). This was a post World War II pinwheel calculator manufactured in Germany (c.1950). Serial number: 25,357. Availability: Scarce. Value: $200.

Reuters Saxonia. This stepped drum arithmometer was the same machine as the original Saxonia. It was distributed in the United States under the name of "Reuters Multiplying and Dividing Machine" of Philadelphia, Pennsylvania. It is shown with the German patents: DRGM 394,014 and 829,403. Like the third model of the Saxonia, it had a wood case with collapsible sides and a sliding top that worked like a tambour on a roll top desk. It had six setting levers that swung in an arc; seven positions in the revolution counter and twelve positions in the result mechanism. (c.1895) Serial number: 3,095. Availability: Rare. Value: $7,500.

Rheinmetall (Full-Keyboard). A full-keyboard German calculator, first appearing on the market in 1924 and manufactured by Rheinische Metall-Handelsgesellschaft. Serial number: 102,935. Availability: Common. Value: $175.

Rheinmetall

Rheinmetall (Ten-Key). A ten-key keyboard with printing mechanism. An early electric with an outboard motor. Serial number: 16,699. Availability: Scarce. Value: $125.

Saxonia (Model 1). Manufactured by Rechenmasch Workstatt Saxonia, Glashütte, i/s. Introduced in 1895 by former employee's of the Burkhardt Arithmometer Company. The mechanical principle used in the Saxonia was of the type known as the "stepped drum." Gottfried Wilhelm Leibniz originally invented this principle. As early as 1673, he submitted drawings and plans for his calculating mechanism. The Model 1 pictured has ten setting slides; twenty places in the result mechanism and eleven places in the revolution counter. Located in the extreme upper left and right hand corners is the knob that cleared the result and revolution counters. Availability: Rare. Value: $5,000.

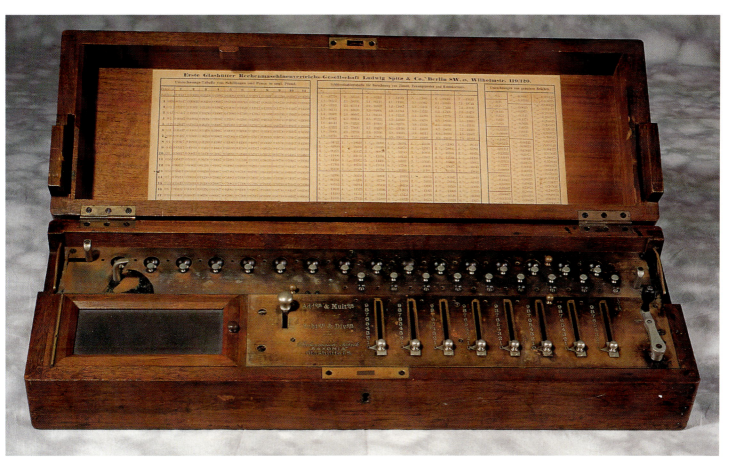

Saxonia (Model 2). The Model 2 is similar to their Model 1 except that the clearing knobs have been changed to levers and it has sixteen places in the result mechanism, nine places in the revolution counter, and eight setting slides. Engraved on the faceplate is the following: "Rechenmasch Fabrik, Saxonia, Glashütte i/s." On the inside top cover the following is printed: "Erste Glashütter, Rechenmaschenenvertriebs – Gesellshaft Ludwig Spitz & Company, Berlin SW 48, Wilkelmstr. 119/20. Agents: Spectator Co., 135 William St., of New York, NY, distributed in the United States." Serial number: 8,444. Availability: Rare. Value: $4,000.

Saxonia (Model 3). The outside case was changed on this model. It had collapsible sides and a sliding top, similar to a tambour on a roll-top desk. Instead of setting levers, it had 6 rotating-type lever controls. The result mechanism had twelve places. This same machine appears under the name "Reuters Multiplying and Division Machine," shown previously as the "Reuters Saxonia." Availability: Rare. Value: $7,500.

Schickard. The Schickard calculator dates back to the year 1623 and is thought to be the first calculating machine. There are no known machines to exist and only a drawing by Schickard has been found. The example is a reproduction that was crafted by Peter Roubos of the Netherlands. Availability: Scarce. Value: $400.

Solo. A small plastic adding machine made in Japan. Also manufactured under the name Chadwick. Availability: Common. Value: $15.

Spalding. An unusual adding machine that was invented by C. G. Spalding with patents of January 13, 1874 and February 19, 1884. The unit is enclosed in a wooden frame and has nine setting levers and two clock like dials for hundreds and units. Serial number: 723. Availability: Rare. Value: $8,500.

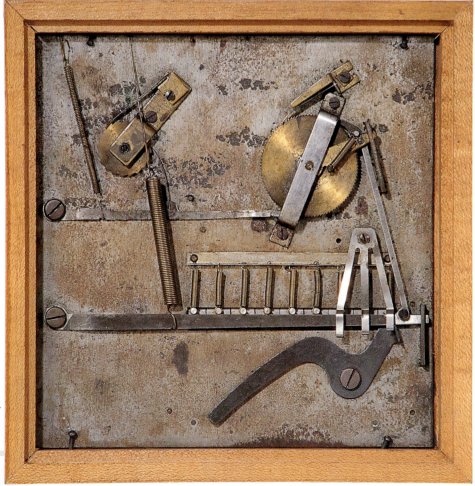

Spalding Mechanism.

114 Standard

Standard (Model B). One of those very attractive adding machines in which the manufacturer was so proud of the quality of his work that he put glass front and sides on it so that you could see the quality of the internal mechanism at work. A small key unlocked the front panel so that it could be easily removed in order to change the paper tape. Standard reported it to be the first 10-key printing adding machine. It was patented in 1891 and appeared on the market in 1903. However, Remington advertised the Dalton adding machine as the first ten-key printing adding machine. It was patented in 1902. Since it did not have the decimal tab preset keys, the operator was able to use a faster touch and this is undoubtedly why the Dalton was so successful. The Standard Model B operated in a similar fashion to the ten-key decimal tabulator on a typewriter. The top row of keys positioned the operator in the column she wished to add (from left to right). The second row of numbered keys or bottom row, were the keys used to input the number desired. The Standard Adding Machine Company of St. Louis, Missouri manufactured it. Patent dates: March 3, 1891; March 27, 1894 and October 8, 1901. Availability: Scarce. Value: $650.

Starr. Manufactured by the Todd Protectograph Company of Rochester, New York. Originally appeared under the name AMCO - an acronym for "Accounting Machine Company" (c.1922) Availability: Common. Value: $35.

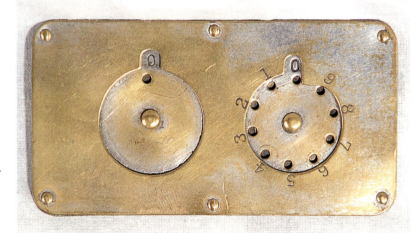

Stephenson (Model A). A small cogged wheel disk-type adder with a plain front plate. On the reverse side of adder is marked "C. B. Simmons, Gen'l Agent, Oil City, Pennsylvania." Patented on March 25, 1873. Availability: Common. Value: $50.

Stephenson (Model B). A very small cogged disk adder of the Pascal principle. The front cover of this model has a decorative trim around the two disks and on the back is printed the following: "A. M. Stephenson Company of Joliet, Illinois, Agents wanted." (c.1900) Availability: Common. Value: $75.

Sumit. Manufactured by the Pearl Engraving Corporation at 29 East 19th Street of New York. Availability: Common. Value: $10.

Sumaster. A stylus-operated vertical cogged slide bar palm-size adder and also capable of addition and subtraction. Availability: Common. Value: $5.

Summator. Hans Sabielny, Dresden, Germany, manufactured this small hand-held stylus-operated calculator in 1921. Serial number: 830. Availability: Scarce. Value: $300.

Sumax-E. *See Addimult.*

Sundstrand   117

Sundstrand. Manufactured by the Sundstrand Adding Machine Company of Rockford, Illinois. Introduced in 1914 and invented by Oskar Sundstrand. A 10-key keyboard with results that were visible on a printed tape at the top of the machine. Proved to be a mechanically sound machine. The Underwood Corporation eventually purchased it. Availability: Common. Value: $35.

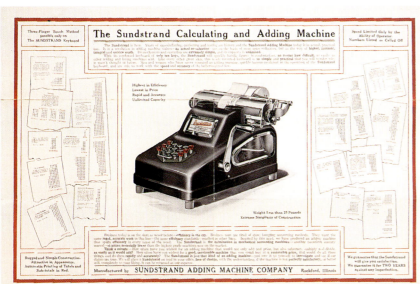

Swift

Swift (A). A ten-key hand-operated adder manufactured by Swift Business Machines of Great Barrington, Massachusetts. Serial number: 925,867. Availability: Common. Value: $25.

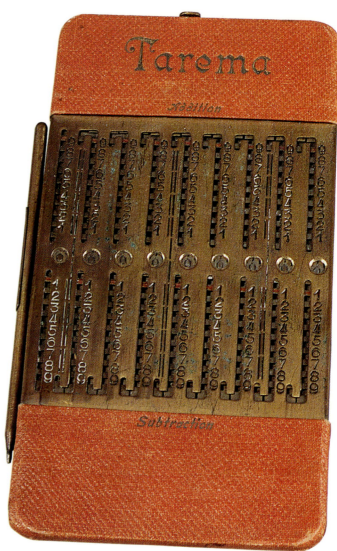

Tarema. A small hand-held stylus-type adder and subtracter. Availability: Common. Value: $10.

Swift (B). This hand calculator is more of a toy. It uses a stylus and has seven places in the setting and result mechanism. Made in Hong Kong. Availability: Common. Value: $10.

Tasco. Also called a Pocket Arithmometer. It is identical to the Cray adder. Availability: Common. Value: $10.

Below:
Tate Arithmometer. The Tate Arithmometer was an improved version of the Layton Arithmometer of 1883. Tate marketed the improved version beginning in 1907. The face of the machine is engraved with the inscription, "Tates Improved Arithmometer 1903 Patent." A label on the inside cover of the machine reads as follows: "S. Tate, Patentee and Sole Maker, London. 29 Fredrick Street, Grays Inn Road." Availability: Rare. Value: $5,500.

Thomas de Colmar. Charles Xavier Thomas de Colmar (1785-1870) was the inventor of this calculator and is considered by many to be the person most responsible for the growth of the calculator industry. The above example of an early Thomas machine has a serial number 725. It has eight setting levers, nine revolution counters, and sixteen places in the result mechanism. (c.1850) Availability: Rare. Value: $10,000.

Tiger. A Japanese pinwheel calculator that resembles the Brunsviga-type machine. Availability: Scarce. Value: $350.

TIM

The name of the TIM calculator was an acronym for "Time Is Money." This was a stepped-drum machine that was manufactured by the Ludwig Spitz & Company of Berlin, Germany. The first model was introduced in 1907 with a wooden case or frame. The availability of this machine is rare and the value is approximately $5,500. In 1909, a heavy cast iron frame machine appeared with eight setting levers and sixteen digits in the result mechanism.

TIM (Lever-set Model). Serial number: 6,331. Availability: Scarce. Value: $500.

TIM (Key-top Model). Serial number: 06,080. Availability: Scarce. Value: $400.

Time Computer. Manufactured by the H. H. Allison Company of Sac City, Iowa. A device used to compute current calendar days and expired and unexpired days in any given month. Serial number: 80. Availability: Scarce. Value: $75.

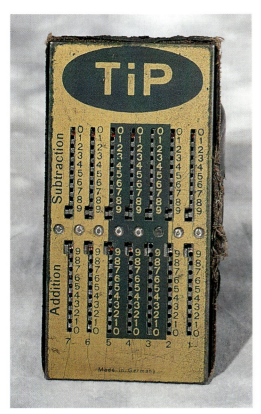

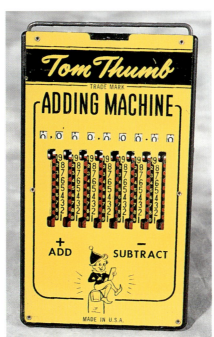

Tom Thumb. Stylus-operated vertical cogged slide bar which was also capable of addition and subtraction. Made in USA. Availability: Common. Value: $5.

TIP. A stylus-operated vertical cogged slide bar which was also capable of addition and subtraction. Availability: Common. Value: $5.

Above and left:
Torpedo. Manufactured by Schnell Addiermaschine, Torpedo Werke A.G. Frankfurt AM. A German adding machine with only 5 (five) keys in a column. Bakelite case. (c.1945) Availability: Scarce. Value: $200.

124 Tower Adding Machine

Tower Adding Machine. Tower was a trade name used by Sears Roebuck and Company. Availability: Common. Value: $15.

Triumph (Model A). Manufactured by the Triumph Precision Machine Company located at 74 Wall Street in New York, New York. The Triumph was a relatively simple adding machine with only four working parts. It has a unique numerical entry system whereby the operator places a finger on the key desired and pulls down a chain link as far as it will go. Machines were made for both American and English markets. Patented February 12, 1907. Serial number: 1,057. (c.1910) Availability: Rare. Value: $1,800.

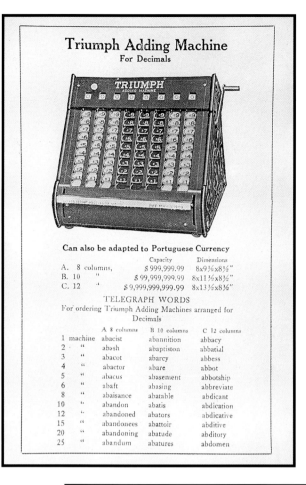

Triumph Adding Machine
For Decimals

Can also be adapted to Portuguese Currency

	Capacity	Dimensions
A. 8 columns,	$ 999,999.99	8x9½x8½"
B. 10 "	$ 99,999,999.99	8x11½x8½"
C. 12 "	$ 9,999,999,999.99	8x13½x8½"

TELEGRAPH WORDS
For ordering Triumph Adding Machines arranged for Decimals

		A 8 columns	B 10 columns	C 12 columns
1	machine	abacist	abannition	abbacy
2	"	abash	abaptiston	abbatial
3	"	abacot	abarcy	abbess
4	"	abactor	abare	abbot
5	"	abacus	abasement	abbotship
6	"	abaft	abasing	abbreviate
8	"	abaisance	abatable	abdicant
10	"	abandon	abatis	abdication
12	"	abandoned	abators	abdicative
15	"	abandonees	abattoir	abditive
20	"	abandoning	abatude	abditory
25	"	abandum	abatures	abdomen

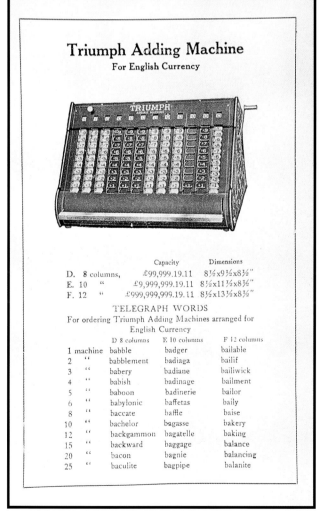

Triumph Adding Machine
For English Currency

	Capacity	Dimensions
D. 8 columns,	£99,999.19.11	8½x9½x8½"
E. 10 "	£9,999,999.19.11	8½x11½x8½"
F. 12 "	£999,999,999.19.11	8½x13½x8½"

TELEGRAPH WORDS
For ordering Triumph Adding Machines arranged for English Currency

		D 8 columns	E 10 columns	F 12 columns
1	machine	babble	badger	bailable
2	"	babblement	badiaga	bailif
3	"	babery	badiane	bailiwick
4	"	babish	badinage	bailment
5	"	baboon	badinerie	bailor
6	"	babylonic	baffetas	baily
8	"	baccate	baffle	baise
10	"	bachelor	bagasse	bakery
12	"	backgammon	bagatelle	baking
15	"	backward	baggage	balance
20	"	bacon	bagnie	balancing
25	"	baculite	bagpipe	balanite

Triumph Adding Machine
With Fractions

Can be adapted to any System of Fractions desired

TELEGRAPH WORDS
For ordering Triumph Adding Machines with Eighths

		S. 8 columns	S. 10 columns	S. 12 columns
1	machine	sabadilla	sabeism	sackage
2	"	sabbatarian	sabelliat	sackful
3	"	sabbath	sabian	sacker
4	"	sabbatic	sabianism	sacking
5	"	sabbatism	sabine	sacrate

For ordering Triumph Adding Machines with Twelfths

		S. 8 columns	S. 10 columns	S. 12 columns
1	machine	scabbard	scallion	scandalous
2	"	scabrous	scallop	scandalum
3	"	scaffling	scalps	scandent
4	"	scaffold	scalpel	scansion
5	"	scalable	scalping	scansorial

Triumph company brochures. There were three models of the Triumph Adding Machine as illustrated in the three company brochures above. There was the decimal model, which was available in 8, 10, or 12-column capacity. The model for English currency was also available in 8,10,or 12 column. And, finally the model designed for fractions with 8, 10, or 12-column capacity. Availability (each machine): Rare. Value (per pictured machine): $2,000.

126 Underwood Sundstrand

Underwood Sundstrand (Model 8120). Manufactured by the Underwood Corporation. Originally produced by the Sundstrand Adding Machine Company of Rockford, Illinois. (c.1914) Serial number: 546,957. Availability: Common. Value: $50.

Unitas. Manufactured by Ludwig Spitz and Company, Ltd., Berlin, Tempelhof, Eresburgerstr. This model has two counting mechanisms. Both have sixteen places in the result and registers. It has eight setting levers and nine places in the revolution counter. The serial number of this unit is 549, which indicates that it is a very early model. It has beveled glass sides and back. The front panel has the name "Unitas" cut out. Availability: Rare. Value: $3,000.

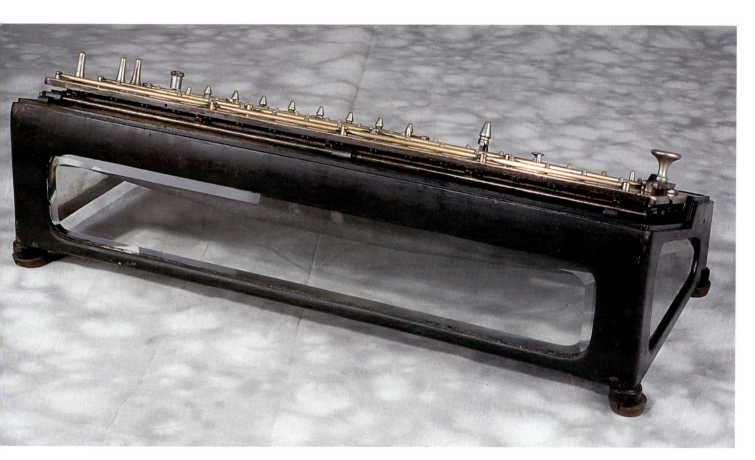

Universal

Universal. Manufactured by the Universal Adding Machine Company at 358 Pearl Street in New York, New York. Patent date: July 15, 1890. A sliding bar action in which an operator, using a stylus, can add by moving numbers to the right and then reading the result on the reverse side. Availability: Rare. Value: $1,000.

Unknown Adder. This is an interesting adding machine. Unfortunately the manufacturer is unknown at the present time. It was probably never put on the market. It is a ten-key printing hand-operated adder. An unusual feature of the machine is that as a key is depressed, a graduated sliding bar incrementally moves out of the left side of the machine. Availability: Rare. Value: $1,500.

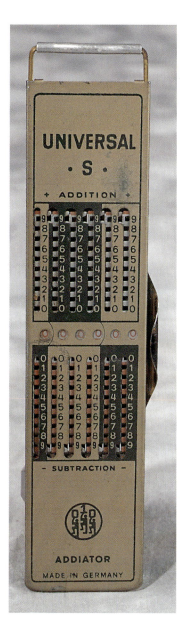

Universal-S. Manufactured by the Addiator Company of Germany. A stylus-operated cogged vertical slide bar action with addition and subtraction. Availability: Common. Value: $5.

Right:
Valiant. A Japanese version of the stylus-operated vertical cogged slide bar capable of addition and subtraction. Availability: Common. Value: $5.

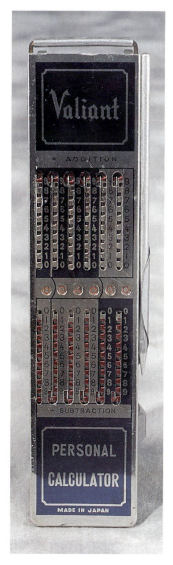

Ve-Po-Ad

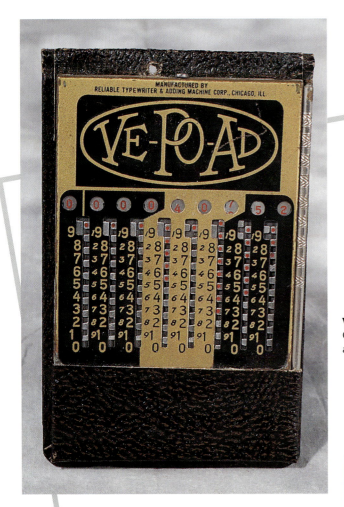

Ve-Po-Ad. Manufactured by the Reliable Typewriter and Adding Machine Corporation of Chicago, Illinois. A stylus-operated cogged vertical slide bar adder with addition and subtraction. Availability: Common. Value: $5.

an Adding Machine in Your Pocket!

● "It can't be true," you say—but it IS true! It is a fact that you can now have an adding machine which will ADD, SUBTRACT and MULTIPLY with a capacity of ONE BILLION—and that you can carry this machine right in your pocket.

You would like an adding machine, wouldn't you? Everybody does—even for use in the home—but how many people can afford to purchase an expensive machine! VE-PO-AD is an amazing invention and is sold for only $2.95. And best of all—it is sent to you on ten days trial. Order one —or several of them now. Try them for ten days and if you don't find them to be accurate, convenient and satisfactory in every respect—return them and your money, less postage, will be refunded to you promptly. VE-PO-AD is built upon a basic, mathematical principle, which insures absolute accuracy. It would be impossible to estimate the number of uses for VE-PO-ADS. Stores, offices, factories, lawyers, doctors, clubs— all who use figures are prospects.

No Need to Make Costly Errors

Now that you can have a VE-PO-AD for only $2.95, there is no need to take the risk of making costly mistakes with figures. With a VE-PO-AD you can extend invoices, check up on costs and do practically everything that an average adding machine will do. Remember that in addition to adding—VE-PO-ADS subtract and multiply—and do all of these accurately. You can think of dozens and dozens of uses for a VE-PO-AD —especially when you consider that it weighs only a few ounces and can be carried easily in your pocket. There are hundreds of opportunities to make money selling VE-PO-ADS—for most everybody who sees one, wants it.

Salesmen Make Over 100% Profit

You will find our policy, as to salesmen's profits, extra-liberal—for we want you to make money—make a lot of money . . . by selling these machines. Even if you intend to devote only a part of your time to this work, you will find it very profitable—for our discounts are large, even if purchases are made in small quantities. Look at the prices quoted you in our letter. Then send in for trial order.

Fully Guaranteed

Every VE-PO-AD is guaranteed to be mechanically correct. Every one is guaranteed to be accurate. VE-PO-ADS are made of etched brass and covered with long-wear leatherette—and with ordinary care should last a long time. Furthermore, you take no risks when ordering for if you do not sell your first order of VE-PO-ADS in ten days, return them and your money will be promptly refunded.

Send Trial Order Now on Money Back Offer

HERE'S THE MACHINE

Only ⅜" thick
This lever clears machine
Face of etched brass
Length 5 inches
Handsome leatherette cover

- Adds up to $9,999,999.99
- Absolutely accurate
- Adds—Subtracts—Mutiplies
- Saves mistakes in figuring
- Total—always visible
- Handsomely finished in etched brass
- Covered with long-wear leatherette
- Operates easily
- Very fast
- Clears instantly

VE-PO-AD Division of Reliable Typewriter and Adding Machine Co.
303 WEST MONROE ST., CHICAGO, ILL.

Advertising, "Saturday Evening Post," October 23, 1926

Advertising, "Saturday Evening Post," October 4, 1952

Oliver Johantgen invented the first Victor Adding Machine and started the Victor Adding Machine Company on March 8, 1918. However, the company was so under capitalized that the first machine had not been manufactured. It was not manufactured until Carl Buehler, the owner of a chain of meat markets, became interested. After giving his financial support, Buehler was elected as the company's first President.

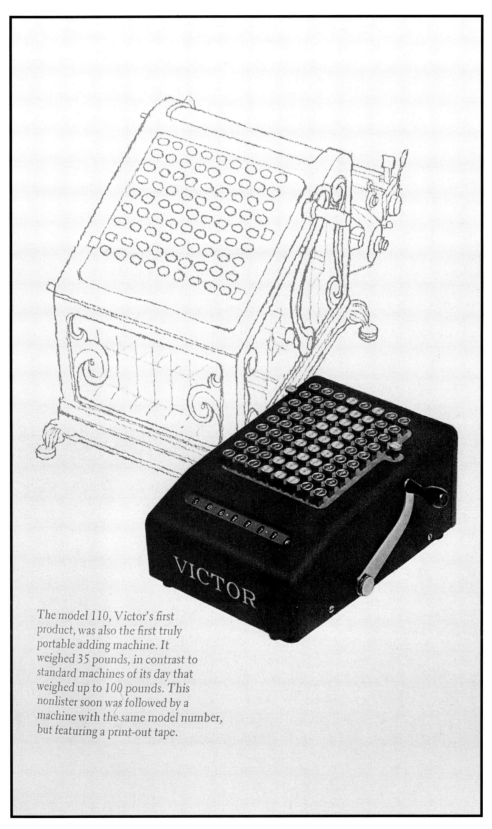

The model 110, Victor's first product, was also the first truly portable adding machine. It weighed 35 pounds, in contrast to standard machines of its day that weighed up to 100 pounds. This nonlister soon was followed by a machine with the same model number, but featuring a print-out tape.

Victor (Model 110)

Victor's first adding machine was the Model 110. It was first produced in 1918. It was a non-printing adding machine. Later, in 1921, a paper tape version of the Model 110 was introduced. It proved to be very successful. During the first year of manufacture, over 2,000 machines were sold. The following year, Buehler signed a contract to deliver 1,000 Model 110's to the McCaskey Cash Register Company.

By 1928, Victor had successfully established over 400 dealers to market their adding machines and had developed a close dealer-manufacturer relationship. This was evidenced by a bold offer made to their dealers. That offer stated that if any dealers weren't completely satisfied with any Victor adding machine, Victor would take it back. Not one single dealer responded to the offer.

In 1928, Victor introduced its first models that subtracted as well as added: the 310S and the 320S. Even during the depression of 1931, Victor introduced two new models, the electric 511S-12 and the 521S-12. Victor's growth continued and in 1939, the Model 600 and 700 series were announced. The Model 600 was a full-keyboard machine with the 700 a 10-key model. Between 1938 and 1941, Victor's sales increased by 301 percent.

During World War II, like so many other manufacturers, Victor converted its factories to the war effort. One of the items they produced was the highly secretive Mark XV, Model 7, Norden Bomb sight.

By 1947, Victor was back to producing adding machines in a big way. It manufactured and sold 8,755,000 units to become the largest exclusive manufacturer of adding machines. In 1953, Victor purchased the McCaskey Register Company and for the first time entered the Cash Register market. In 1954, the first automatic printing calculator was placed on the market.

In 1961, the famous Comptometer Corporation and Victor merged into a publicly traded company called the Victor Comptometer Corporation. Then, in the early 1970s, Victor entered the electronics market with a line of electronic calculators (1971); an electronic dot matrix printer (1973); programmable calculators (1974); and electronic cash registers (1975).

Finally, in 1977 Victor Comptometer Corporation was purchased by Kidde, Inc. and became a wholly owned subsidiary known as Victor Business Products. About the same time Victor introduced a CP/M based desktop computer called the Victor 9000. The 9000 computer remained a best seller until IBM came out with PC-DOS. Like so many other non-compatible operating systems, Victor quickly developed financial troubles. In 1984, they filed for protection under Chapter 11 bankruptcy proceedings.

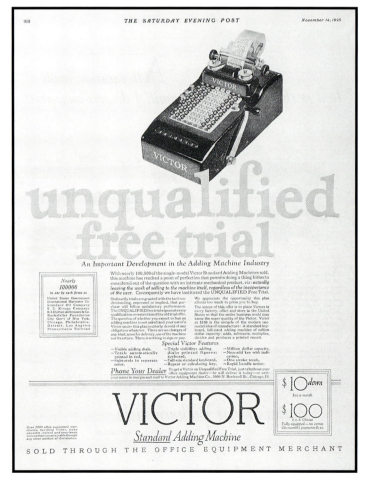

Left and above:
Victor (Model 6). A full-keyboard hand-operated adding machine with printing mechanism. Manufactured by the Victor Adding Machine Company of Chicago, Illinois. Serial number: 320,805 (c.1921) Availability: Common. Value: $50.

Victor. A full-keyboard electric adding machine. Serial number: 356,315. Patented: April 13, 1920. Availability: Common. Value: $75.

Victor

Victor. A ten-key keyboard hand-operated adding machine. Manufactured by the Victor Adding Machine Company of Chicago, Illinois. Serial number: 744,709. It has a Bakelite case. Availability: Common. Value: $25.

Victor (Model Figure-Eight-A). This is not the same Victor Adding Machine Company of Chicago, Illinois. Probably made by Webb with the Victor label. It is nickel-plated. Availability: Rare. Value: $500.

Victor (Model Figure-Eight-B). A figure-eight adder of the Webb type. Brass and nickel-plated. Availability: Rare. Value: $500.

Wales

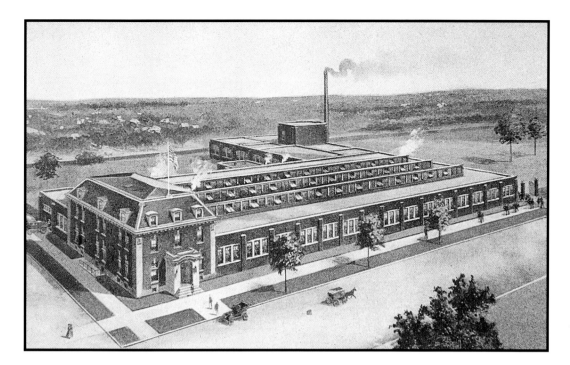

Wales Factory

Wales Detail Assembly Room

Wales Polishing Room

Wales (Model 10). Manufactured by the Wales Adding Machine Company of Wilkes-Barre, Pennsylvania. Later the name was changed to the Adder Machine Company. The Wales was a full-keyboard, visible adding machine that came in a variety of models. The early model had glass front and sides and was very heavy. (c.1903) Serial number: 33,553. Availability: Common. Value: $75.

Wales 139

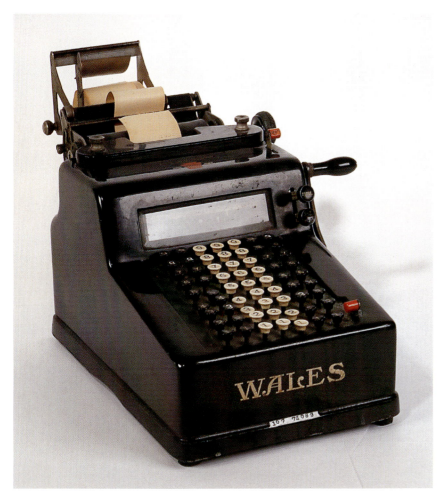

Wales (Model 107). Serial number: 72,089. Availability: Common. Value: $75.

Wales (Model 24). Serial number: 7,380 (Allen-Wales). Availability: Common. Value: $75.

Walther (Model RMKZ). A pinwheel-type calculator that was Manufactured by Carl Walther, Abt. Rechenmaschinen, Zella-Mehlisi. Thür and distributed by Brune & Stock Düsseldorf. Serial number: 10,974. Availability: Scarce. Value: $300.

Wang (Model 320) – Manufactured by Wang Laboratories of Tewksbury, Massachusetts. Serial number: 203,619. Availability: Scarce. Value: $175.

Webb

The Webb Adding Machine sometimes called the *"figure-eight"* adding machine was first patented by Charles Henry Webb on March 10, 1868. Because of Webb's background, you would think he would be more inclined to invent a typewriter than an adding machine. The major part of his life was devoted to a career as an author and a journalist. At the age of seventeen Webb worked for a newspaper in New York. But after reading the novel "Moby Dick" he must have decided he needed more experience. He signed up on a whaling ship and sailed to the South Seas and the Arctic where he spent several years. In 1859, he contributed poems to "Harper's Weekly." In 1860, he worked for the "New York Times," where he wrote a column called "Minor Topics." In 1861, he became a Civil War correspondent and was present at Bull Run as well as the early campaigns in the Shenandoah Valley. From 1863 to 1866, Webb worked for the "San Francisco Evening Bulletin." He became a close friend of Bret Harte and Mark Twain. In 1866, he returned to New York and the following year became the sponsor and publisher of Mark Twain's first short story, "The Celebrated Jumping Frog of Calaveras County." In 1872, he became a broker and banker, but was caught in the financial panic of 1873.

C. H. Webb's first patent, March 10, 1868

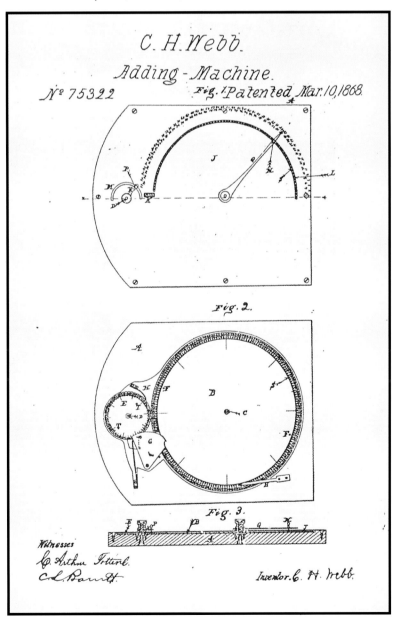

Webb and Webb-types

Shortly after publishing Mark Twain's short story in 1867, Webb became interested in the invention of a small adding device with a rotating numbered disk and multiplying wheel arranged under the dial plate. Webb applied for a patent and on March 10, 1868, patent number 75,322 was granted to him.

The author has in his collection two similar cardboard adding devices. The origin and date of these two devices are unknown, but the similarity is worth bringing to your attention. All Webb-"type" calculating devices are listed together to illustrate the different variations available.

Webb-type (Single and Double). Cardboard adders of unknown origin. Availability: Rare. Value: $600 - $1,200.

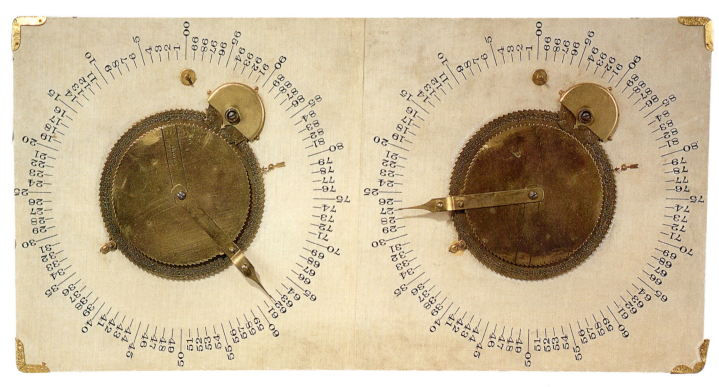

Webb's first product was different from his approved patent. The face was brass and was attached to a wood base resembling a figure 8. It was called "The Adder" and referred to his first patent of 1868.

Webb's "The Adder" (Webb Variation A). Patented March 10, 1868. Availability: Rare. Value: $700.

Webb's "The Adder" (Webb Variation B). Patented March 10, 1868. This variation has a brass and nickel face-plate which also has a wood base. Availability: Rare. Value: $900.

144   Webb and Webb-types

Webb's "The Adder" (Webb Variation C). Patent dates on this version are November 5th & 12th, 1889. The specimen pictured is housed in a wood carrying case with a stylus. Availability: Rare. Value: $800.

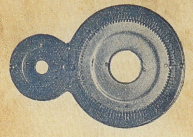

Left and above:
Lightning (Webb Variation D). This version is identical to the 1889 version except it has no name or patent dates on the face. Since it was still in its original labeled box it was identified as a Lightning. Availability: Scarce. Value: $500.

Webb and Webb-types 145

Victor (Webb Variations E & F). Both of these versions are marked with the name Victor. One is all nickel-plated and the other is brass and nickel. There are no other markings on either unit. Availability: Scarce. Value: Each: $500.

DIRECTIONS FOR USING THE
VICTOR ADDING MACHINE

We will suppose that we have a column of figures as follows:
4212
6123
4532
1436
2242

First set the machine at zero by placing the pointer at 0 in the large dial and turning it to the stopping point. Turn the small wheel to 0 by placing the pointer in the small hole and turning it to the stopping point.

Now, commence and add the first two columns, using the large dial. To add rapidly it is just as easy to add combinations of figures as to turn the dial for each amount. For instance, starting at the top of the column, it is just as easy to see that the first two amounts equal 35 as to turn the dial for each amount separately. Consequently, place the pointer at 35 and turn to the stopping point.

The next two amounts equal 68. Place the pointer at 68 and turn to the stopping point.

The next amount is 42. Place the pointer at 42 and turn to the stopping point.

The machine now shows a total of 145. Put down 45 and we have 1 to carry.

Now turn the machine to 0 again and proceed to add the next two columns. Having had 1 to carry, we consequently place the pointer at 43, which includes the first amount of 42 at the top and the 1 we had to carry.

Now add 61, then 59, then 22.

The machine now shows 185. Put this amount under the columns and we have 18,545 for the total.

We will now take an example of five columns. Use the same figures as in the foregoing illustration, except that we will add 2 to the first amount, 7 to the second, 8 to the third, 9 to the fourth, and 5 to the fifth.

We will proceed as in the other example, first adding the first two columns, which gives us a total of 145.

Put down 45 and carry 1 to the next column, which will give us 243 to be added first.

Put the pointer at 2 in the small dial, and turn to the stopping point, when 200 will be shown.

Then put the pointer at 43 in the large dial, and turn to the stopping point, which gives us 43.

Next place the pointer at 7 in the small dial, 61 in the large, etc., until the amounts have been added.

The machine will then show a total of 3,285. Put this under the column and we have a total of 328,545, which is the correct amount of the whole column.

Kueffel & Esser (Webb Variation G). This unit is marked with the 1889 patent dates of November 5th & 12th embedded in a steel rectangular frame. A metal label in the upper left hand corner is inscribed as follows: "J. L. Herring's Computing Machine; Keuffel & Esser Company, New York; Sole Agents for the United States and Canada." It has a number 10 punched on the rear side. Availability: Scarce. Value: $500.

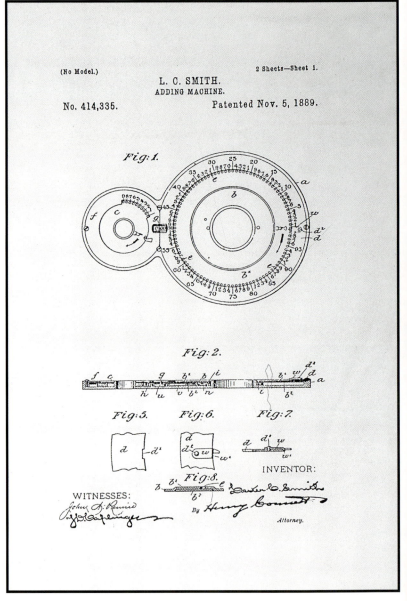

L. C. Smith (Webb Variation I). This is the patent drawing and while the actual machine has surfaced at auctions and private sales, it has not been found by the author. It has been reported that Webb acquired this patent from Smith.

Herring, J. L. (Webb Variation H). Marked "J. L. Herring's Computing Machine, Derry, PA (Westmoreland County)." Serial number: 30,500. On the lower right hand corner is printed "Train-Resistance Tons." Herring's patent numbers are embedded in the cast iron base. It has a setting control slide that is movable. Availability: Rare. Value: $500.

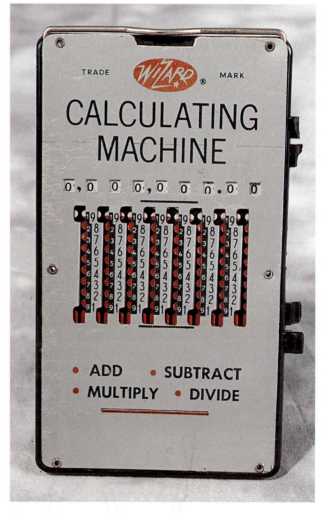

Wizard Calculating Machine. A stylus-operated adder with a vertical cogged slide bar action. This machine was capable of addition and subtraction. The manufacturer claimed that it could also perform multiplication and division. Availability: Common. Value: $5.

Counting Machines

Counters, as distinguished from adding machines, are designed specifically for one application, to simply register one whole number for each item counted. As a rule, counters are simple mechanical devices that cannot subtract, multiply, or divide.

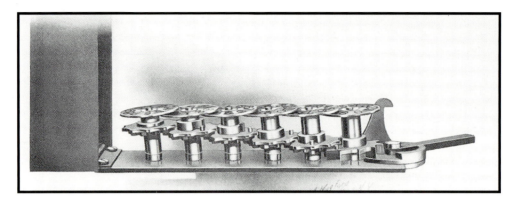

Counter Mechanism. A typical mechanism that consists of 6 posts that represent columns. Each post has a sprocket that is offset with a pivot bar that is tripped when all nine digits have been indexed, thereby causing the next column or columns to register, resulting in a tens-carry action.

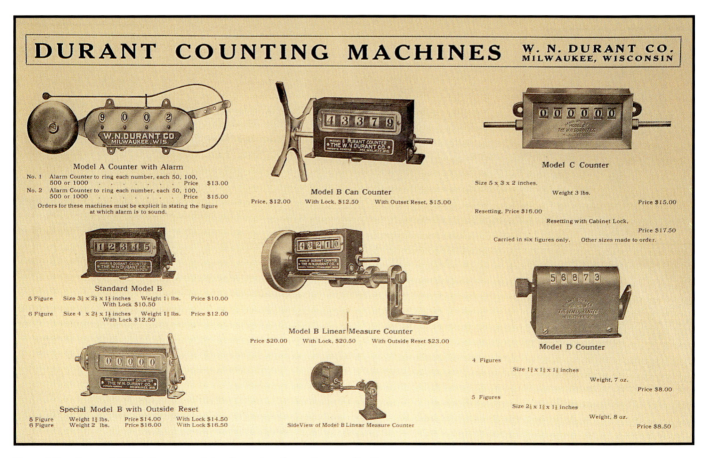

Durant Brochure of 1915 shows a variety of counters for various applications.

American Counter. Manufactured by the F. B. Redington Company of Chicago, Illinois. (c.1915) Availability: Common. Value: $35.

The C. J. Root Company. This was the C. J. Root Factory in Bristol, Connecticut in 1913. As indicated they manufactured the Bristol counters; the Elm City counters and the Roco counters.

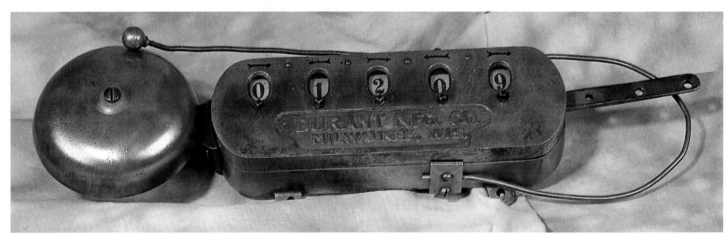

Durant Counter (Model A with alarm). W. N. Durant Manufacturing Company of Milwaukee, Wisconsin. Availability: Scarce. Value: $250.

Elm City Counter (a). Manufactured by the C. J. Root Company of Bristol, Connecticut. Patented in 1891. Availability: Common. Value: $55.

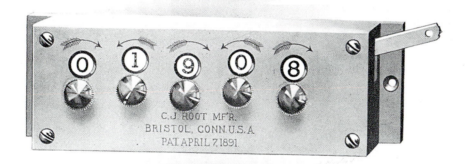

Illustration shows a No. 5, or Five Figure "Elm City" Counter, which counts to 100,000.

ONE-HALF ACTUAL SIZE.

	Size	Shipping weight		Counts		
No. 2.	3¼ x 1¾ x ⅝ ins.	12 ozs.	"	100	-	List price, $4.50
No. 3.	4 x 1¾ x ⅝ "	15 "	"	1,000	-	" 6.00
No. 4.	4¾ x 1¾ x ⅝ "	18 "	"	10,000	-	" 8.00
No. 5.	5½ x 1¾ x ⅝ "	21 "	"	100,000	-	" 10.00
No. 6.	6¼ x 1¾ x ⅝ "	24 "	"	1,000,000	-	" 12.00

Number of Counter corresponds with number of figures.

Sent by mail to any address on receipt of price.

THE C. J. ROOT CO., BRISTOL, CONN.

Elm City

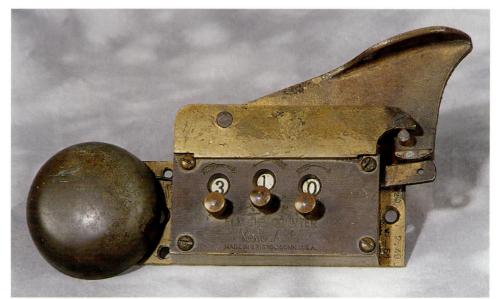

Elm City Counter (b). Manufactured by Veeder-Root Company of Bristol, Connecticut. Hand-activated with alarm or bell. Availability: Scarce. Value: $185.

'O' Tally. Benton Manufacturing Company of New York. A small hand tally. Availability: Common. Value: $25.

Silver-King. Manufactured by the Production Instrument Company of Chicago, Illinois. Availability: Common. Value: $35.

Unknown. Manufacturer is not known but it is believed to be a gate- or turn-style tally. Availability: Scarce. Value: $50.

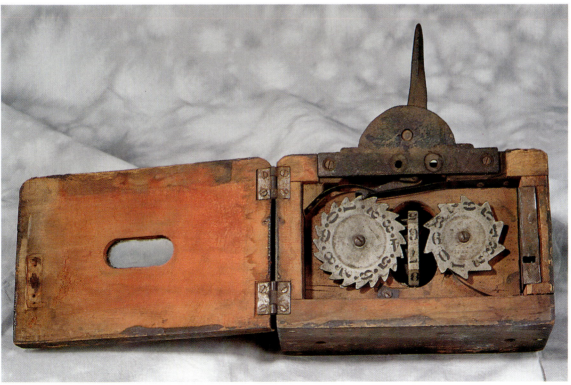

Chapter Three
Combination Adding Machines and Cash Drawers

At the turn of the twentieth century, adding machine manufacturers began to realize that they had the resources to be part of the lucrative cash register market. By placing their adding machine on a cash drawer and designing a simple mechanism that tied the opening of the drawer to the depression of the hand crank, they effectively created a cash register. It was simple, a lot less expensive and capable of several features that were well received by all the small neighborhood grocery stores.

The most popular adding machine combination registers were the listing or printed tape machines. They not only provided a printed record of each transaction for the proprietor, but when used with a carbon paper tape, also provided a copy for the customer.

The printed tape machines were available in either *simplex* or *duplex* models. The simplex model had a single counter and a single detail strip that gave a total for each transaction. The duplex model was available with either a single or double detail strip, but it also had an accumulated grand total. This important feature enabled the end-user to have a total of all transactions at the end of the day.

Some adding machine combination registers could accomplish additional tasks, i.e. include the clerks initials for each transaction; the department involved; the kind of transaction and even the date it all took place.

Every grocer on every block, as well as every service station at each intersection seemed to have an adding machine combination register. As a result, thousands were sold and they can still be found in flea markets and other antique market places.

Add-Index Adding Machine/Cash Drawer Combination Register (Model 5D). Manufactured by the Add-Index Corporation of New York at their factory in Grand Rapids, Michigan. The American Adding Machine Company of Chicago, Illinois, originally placed this machine on the market in 1914. This particular model was placed on a cash drawer manufactured by the Toronto Cash Register Company of Toronto, Ontario, Canada. Serial number: 70,989. Availability: Scarce. Value: $125.

American Calculator Adding Machine/Cash Drawer Combination (Model A). Manufactured by the American Adding Machine Company of 35 South Dearborn Street in Chicago, Illinois. This was the non-listing machine version and was basically the American Model 5 on a cash drawer base. Availability: Common. Value: $125.

American Calculator Adding Machine/Cash Drawer Combination Register (Model B). This is the listing version of the American, which used the Model 4 adding machine on a cash drawer. (c.1928) Availability: Scarce. Value: $150.

Automatic Bookkeeping Register. Manufactured by the Automatic Bookkeeping Register Company of Kansas City, Missouri. This was truly a combination machine. It functioned as an adding machine, a cash register, and a bookkeeping machine. A unique idea when it was first patented on March 31, 1908. After William Laughlin acquired the patent he then formed the Automatic Bookkeeping Register Company. Laughlin also built the brass machine pictured at left. On display at the 1915 Pan American Exposition, it won a Gold Medal. Based on this accomplishment, Laughlin sold stock to raise money to build the production model also shown below. It was all nickel-plated and, unfortunately, weighed 300 pounds. Availability (brass machine): Rare. Value: $5,000. Availability (nickel-plated machine): Rare. Value: $400-$600.

Automatic Bookkeeping Register. A frustrated Sales Manager trying to figure out how he was going to sell a machine that not only weighed 300 pounds but also would not fit on most desks and counters.

Burroughs Adding Machine/Cash Drawer Combination Register (Model 9). Manufactured by the Burroughs Adding Machine Company of Detroit, Michigan. Serial number: 1,205,839. Availability: Common. Value: $100.

Dalton Adding Machine/Cash Drawer Combination Register. Manufactured by the Dalton Adding Machine Company of Cincinnati, Ohio. Availability: Common. Value: $125.

International Money Machine. While the International Adding Machine did not sit over a cash drawer, it was a combination machine with great flexibility and deserves to be mentioned here. The inventor of the International was Gustaf Runquist of Terre Haute, Indiana. He was granted United States patent number 1,213,268 on January 23, 1917. The International Money Machine Company of Terre Haute manufactured this adding machine along with other variations. The following are some of the many applications marketed by the innovative management of the International Company.

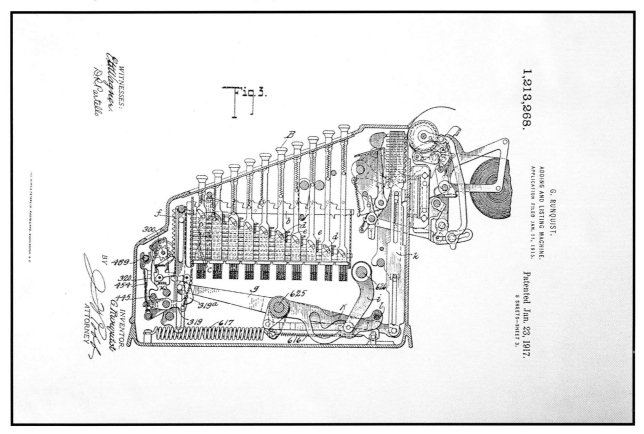

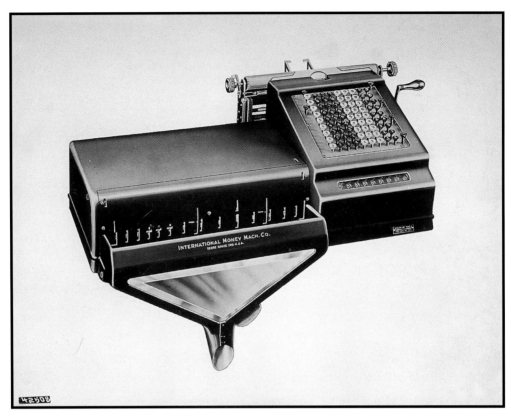

International Payroll and Cashier Machine (Model A). This was a combination adding machine and money paying machine, constructed so that an operator could switch to the independent adding machine by simply depressing a key. The machine pictured here shows the coin tray in position and it is ready to run a payroll.

International Coil-O-Meter (Model B). The attachment pictured shows the several sets of registers or counter wheels allowing for the possibility of counting up to 9,999,999.99 coins of any one denomination.

International Payroll and Cashier Machine (Model C). This view shows the machine with the regular and also the reserve coin tray, which increases its capacity to $20,000.

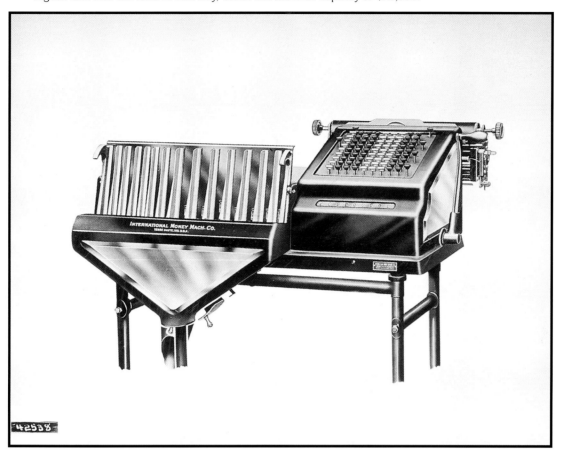

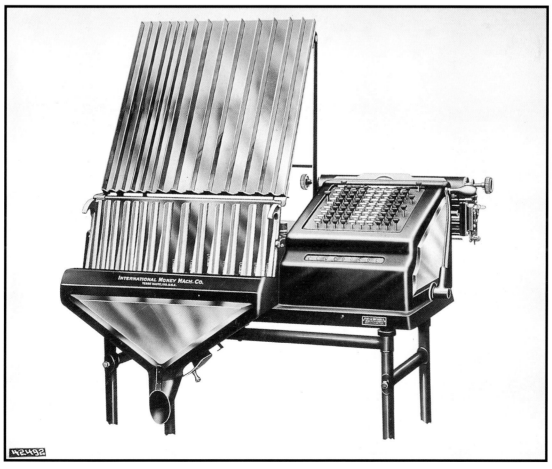

164 International

The following photographs show theses machines in
use by some of the leading companies of the period.

Houghton Oil Company office, Philadelphia, Pennsylvania. Total number of employees was 457; amount of weekly payroll totaled $5,400.68. Two young ladies prepared the payroll in only twenty minutes. The machine not only made the change that went directly into each envelope, but added all the transactions. When the payroll was completed the envelopes were ready for distribution and the auditor had on his desk the printed record of all payments made with "Total Paid Out."

John B. Stetson Hat Co., Philadelphia, Pennsylvania. This company had 4,800 employees and a weekly payroll of $59,754.38.

Hercules Powder Company. These six employees of Hercules are shown with the weekly payroll of $75,867.99 on the table and in the machines. According to the manufacturer they now complete a payroll in one day when it used to take six (6) days.

166   McCaskey

Right and below:
McCaskey Adding Machine Cash Drawer Combination Register. Manufactured by the McCaskey Register Company of Alliance, Ohio. Availability: Common. Value: $75.

Remington Adding Machine Cash Drawer Combination Register. This was the small portable Remington adding machine that was very popular and as a result is very common. However, you don't see it very often on a cash drawer. Availability: Scarce. Value: $100.

Sundstrand Adding Machine Cash Drawer Combination Register. Manufactured by the Sundstrand Adding Machine Company of Rockford, Illinois. Availability: Common. Value: $125.

Underwood Adding Machine Cash Drawer. Manufactured by the Underwood Sundstrand Adding Machine Company. This was an electric adding machine with an outboard motor. Availability: Scarce. Value: $125.

Chapter Four
Combination Adding Machines and Typewriters

Remington Ten-Key Decimal Tabulator Typewriter (Model 7).
Serial number: 167,774. (c.1896) Availability: Scarce. Value: $300.

The Remington Typewriter Company was the first to introduce a feature called *ten-key decimal tab.* It was first available on their Model 7 Typewriter. This feature allowed typists to more easily do columnar work. If an operator wanted to type the number 10,000.00, instead of tabbing to the decimal point and backspacing six times, she would simply touch the 10,000 key and the tabulator would stop at the first figure and automatically line up each decimal point. Some typewriter manufacturers placed the tabulator keys below the space bar similar to the arrangement on the Remington machine. Others felt the tabulator keys should be above the numerals, which seemed to make more sense.

Eventually most of the typewriter manufacturers had the ten-key tab feature and most were located above the numerals. With the ten-key tab feature firmly established it became apparent that columnar work or even accounting functions could be done on the typewriter. It was not until the Union Typewriter Company acquired the exclusive rights to a device called the Wahl Register, that the first combination typewriter and adding machine appeared on the market. The Union Typewriter Company was a trust formed by Remington and other typewriter manufacturers during the early 1920s, in an attempt to control pricing.

Wahl Register

The Wahl Register was attached to the Remington, Monarch, Smith Premier, and Yost. These manufacturers were all part of the aforementioned trust. Basically, the Wahl was attached to the carriage of a typewriter and provided the user with the benefit of adding and/or subtracting vertical columns.

This advertising piece appeared in the *Literary Digest,* April 11, 1914. It shows a picture of the Wahl Register and three of the typewriter companies that were part of the Union Typewriter Company Trust.

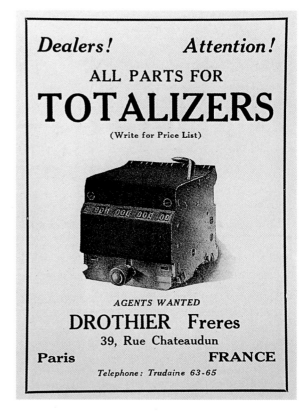

Above and below:
In addition to the Wahl Register, two other registers of the period were the **Totalizer** from Paris, France, and the **Type-Adder** manufactured by the Type-Adder Corporation of New York, New York.

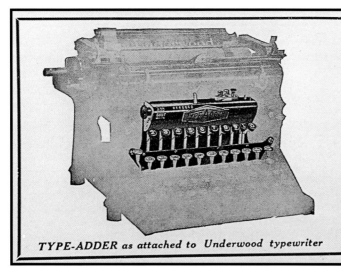

By the late 1920's, Bookkeeping machines not only appeared but had established a special niche in the marketplace. At that time accounting machines were classified into the following categories:

1. Combination Typewriter, Adding and Subtracting Machines:
     Burroughs-Moon Hopkins
     Elliott-Fisher
     Ellis
     Remington
     Underwood
2. Adding Machine Main-Frame with Direct Subtraction and Multiple Totalizers:
     Burroughs
     Dalton
     Ellis
     Sundstrand
3. Typewriter Main-Frame with Adding, Subtracting, Multiplying with Vertical and Cross-Footing Registers:
     Burroughs-Moon Hopkins

These machines replaced the slow drudgery of ledger accounting with pen and ink. Although it took a few years for them to gain acceptance, they became the accounting method of choice for many years.

Burroughs Bookkeeping Machine (Model 13). Manufactured by the Burroughs Adding Machine Company of Detroit, Michigan. Serial number: 1,199,879. Availability: Common. Value: $150.

Dalton Bookkeeping Machine. Manufactured by the Dalton Adding Machine Company of Cincinnati, Ohio. Availability: Scarce. Value: $250.

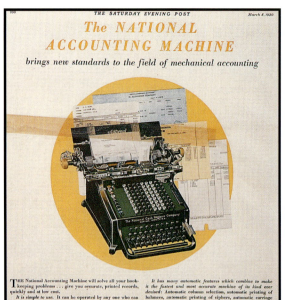

Left and below:

Ellis. A combination adding machine and typewriter that is basically an adding machine with a typewriter attachment. This was a reverse of the combination machines that had surfaced to date. This versatile machine was invented by Halmcolm Ellis of East Orange, New Jersey, and patented in 1906. Its basic mechanism is a full-keyboard adding machine connected to a typewriter mechanism. The result is a machine that is capable of performing arithmetical functions as well as printing alphabetic letters like a typewriter. This combination of functions was referred to as a bookkeeping machine. The specimen pictured came with a tag on it that indicated it was originally the property of the Franklin Institute. (c.1906) Availability: Rare. Value: $3,500.

An Elliott-Fisher brochure and a typical accounting office with a male operator on the Elliott-Fisher bookkeeping machine. (c.1915)

Elliott-Fisher

Elliott-Fisher Bookkeeping Machine. Manufactured by the Elliott Fisher Division of General Office Equipment Corporation of Harrisburg, Pennsylvania. The accounting machine model was equipped with registers mounted on the back, upper carriage assembly. Availability: Scarce. Value: $250.

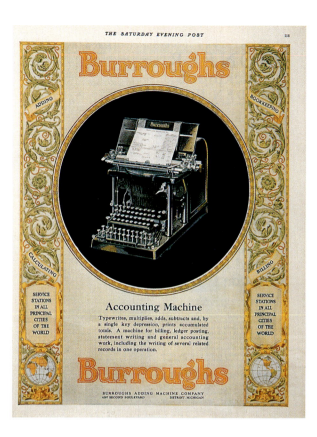

Above and right:
Moon-Hopkins. Hubert Hopkins was the inventor of this adding, typewriter, and bookkeeping machine device and he interested John C. Moon to join him in its manufacture. The Moon Hopkins invention was a combination of a typewriter, a mechanism the equal of four adding machines, and a short-cut multiplier, all in one machine. This machine has a complicated history that involved lawsuits which included the Dalton Adding Machine Company and, later, the Addograph Manufacturing Company and the Addograph Manufacturing Company vs. the Moon-Hopkins Billing Machine Company. Originally the Moon-Hopkins Billing Machine Company of St. Louis, Missouri, manufactured the product. Later, the Burroughs Adding Company manufactured it, but only the electric version. (c.1902-1912) Availability: Rare. Value: $2,000.

Remington Vertical Adder (Model 21). (c.1907) Availability: Scarce. Value: $200.

Below:
Remington Bookkeeping Machine (Model B-85). The B-85 was Remington's first true bookkeeping machine. Availability: Rare. Value: $400.

Underwood 177

Underwood Bookkeeping Machine. Manufactured by the Underwood Typewriter Company, Inc., New York, New York. The manufacturer stated that this machine was a combination typewriter and a built-in computer in the base of the unit. The number of registers on the machine determined the model number. From one to seven registers were available. A standard register had a capacity of nine places or 9,999,999.00 or nine wheels. Machines with 10, 11, or 12 wheels per register were also available. This Underwood model was introduced in 1912. Availability: Rare. Value: $500.

Chapter Five
Slide Rules

Slide rules use a system of mathematics called "Logarithms." A Scottish mathematician, John Napier, first discovered logarithms in 1590. Simply stated logarithms are a method of multiplying and dividing by utilizing addition and subtraction. Napier also is credited with inventing the decimal point or *notation of decimal fractions*. Napier is probably best known for his last published work in the year 1617. Written in Latin, it was called *"Rabdologiae seu numerationis per virgulas libri duo."* The object of his work was to lessen the drudgery of calculations. He defined *Rabdologia* as "numeration by little rods." These little rods, made of bone, ivory or boxwood, were more commonly referred to as "Napier's Bones" and by placing them together in certain combinations, one could perform multiplication and division solutions.

Currently, collectors of *"mathmatica"* will pay as much as $8,000 - $12,000 for an early and complete set of "Napier's Bones." Many reproductions can be attained for a much lesser amount. The following is a reproduction as fabricated by the author.

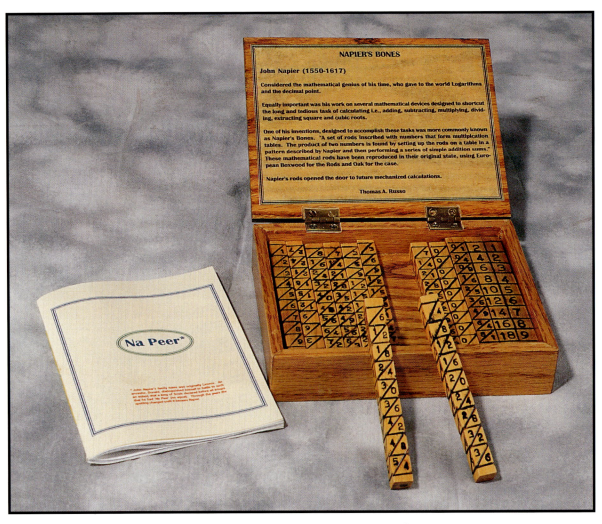

Fabricated reproduction of "Napier's Bones" and instruction book by Thomas A. Russo.

About the year 1600, a mathematician by the name of William Oughtred (1575-1660), conceived the invention of a "projected horizontal instrument for delineating dials upon any kind of plane, and for working most questions that could be performed by the globe." In 1633, William Foster, a pupil of Oughtred's, translated and published a description of Oughtred's invention, together with his own work, called "*Circles of Proportion.*" So, from these beginnings the slide rule was born.

Over the years, the slide rule has taken many forms and shapes and has been the calculator of choice for mathematicians, architects, and engineers up until recent years. In addition to the standard rectangular device, which came in a variety of sizes, there was the circular slide rule, the spherical slide rule and the combination slide rule and adding machine. Some of these devices are described in this chapter. For those of you more interested in slide rules there is an excellent publication called the *Oughtred Society*, published by Robert Otnes of Palo Alto, California.

ACU-MATH Slide Rule Display by Sterling. A display of four Acu-Math slide rules: Model 1211; Model 900; Model 511 (Mannheim Professional); and Model 1311 (Log Log Decimal Trig.) Availability: Scarce. Value: $250.

ALCO (Combination Adder and Slide Rule). Manufactured by ALCO of Japan. Manufacturer literature referred to this device as a "Four-Rule" calculator. The stylus-operated adder on one side handles addition and subtraction with the result shown in the middle. Multiplication is easily and quickly accomplished on the slide rule side of the device. Availability: Scarce. Value: $75.

Atlas Calculator. A circular slide rule manufactured by Gilson Slide Rule Company of Stuart, Florida. Patented January 17, 1922. Made of white enameled aluminum. It is capable of solving problems in multiplication, division, and proportion, and achieving results with a maximum error of less than 1 in 30,000. The Atlas has three scales. The outer scale is the equivalent of a straight slide rule 25" long. The next scale is divided in equal divisions and is used for solving a few types of problems and for quickly locating and factoring on the spiral. The third scale is a spiral having 30 coils. This scale is equivalent to a straight slide rule 60 feet long. The answer to any factor can be read to five positions, i.e. 98,463. Diameter: 8.3125. (c.1924) Availability: Common. Value: $35.

Calculigraphe. A small circular slide rule of French origin. A winding stem that resembles a pocket watch activates the rotary scales. Diameter: 2." Availability: Scarce. Value: $300.

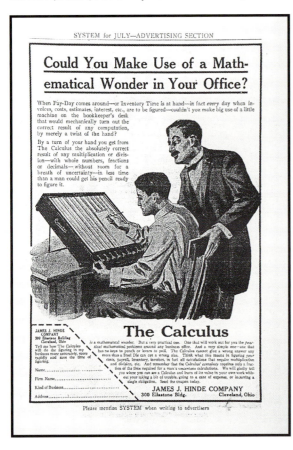

Left and above:
Calculus. Manufactured by the James J. Hinde Company at 300 Ellastone Building in Cleveland, Ohio. Availability: Rare. Value: $900.

Charpentier Calculimètre   181

Above and right:
Charpentier Calculimètre. A French circular metal slide rule invented and manufactured by G. Charpentier, Brevetè S.G.D.G. (c.1900) Diameter: 2.25." An advertisement from the 1913 Kueffel & Esser catalog. Slide rule availability: Scarce. Value: $500.

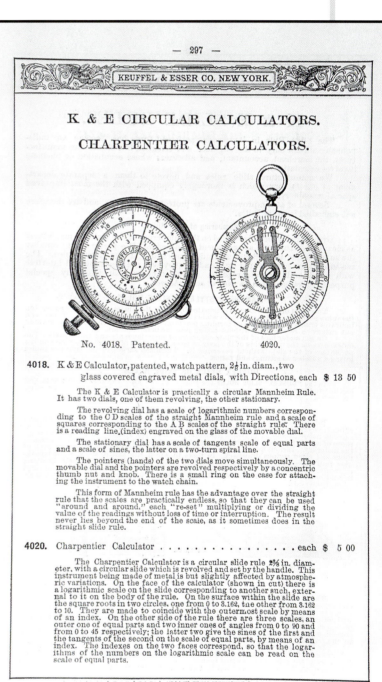

182 Chesterman

Chesterman's Calculator. This device was invented by an Englishman James Chesterman. It was first patented in 1842 and its purpose was to calculate the weight of an animal's four quarters by the use of a tape measure and a circular slide rule. Availability: Scarce. Value: $250.

The operating instructions are interesting and are included for the reader as follows:

Directions: First. Take the length from the foremost right corner of the shoulder blade in a straight line to the hindermost portion of the rump by the tail, and next the xxxxx (word missing) behind the fore-legs. The measures carefully taken will, with the assistance of the circular sliding plate, tell the dead weight of the four quarters, either in the London stone of 8 lbs., the country stone of 14 lbs., or the score of 20 lbs.

Example: suppose the length of the beast to be 5 ft. 6 in. and girth 6 ft. 3 in., turn the slide till the figure 8 with the * is over 5 ft. 6 in. on the inner circle, then look at 6 ft. 3 in. on the slide and over that on the outer circle will be found 90 stones. If the weight be required in stones of 14 lbs. Turn the slide in the same manner til the figure 14 with the * is over the length, when the weight 51 and a half stones will be found over the girth as before. Or if the score of 20 lbs. be required, turn the slide til the figure 20 with the * is over the length, when the weight will be found 36 score."

Faber, A. W. Slide Rule. Made in Germany, D.R.G.M., with serial number 116,832. Has a decimal pointer. Availability: Scarce. Value: $75.

Faber-Castell   183

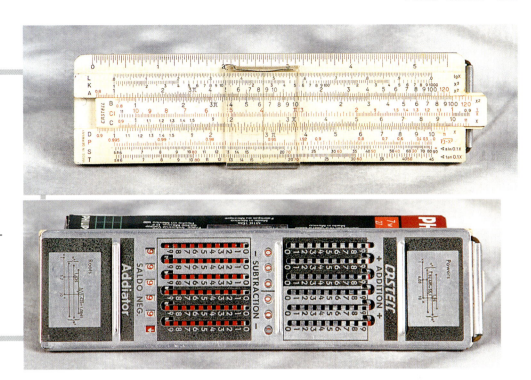

Faber-Castell (Model 6/54Rb).
Manufactured by the Faber-Castell Company of Darnstadt, Germany. A combination Addiator adding machine on one side and a 6" Faber-Castell slide rule on the other side. Availability: Scarce. Value: $150.

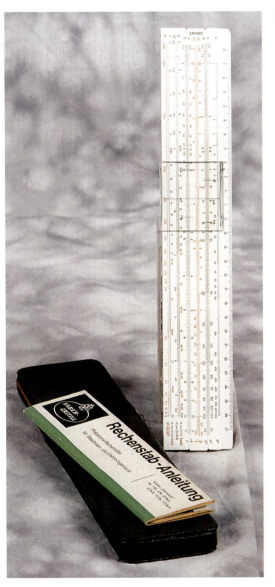
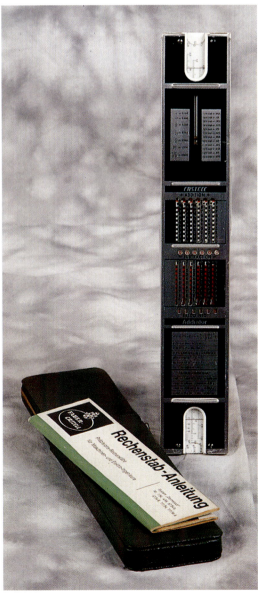

Left and far left:
Faber-Castell (Model 111/54a). Manufactured by Faber-Castell of Darnstadt, Germany. A combination 12" Addiator adding machine on one side and a Faber-Castell slide rule on the other. Availability: Scarce. Value: $250.

Fowler

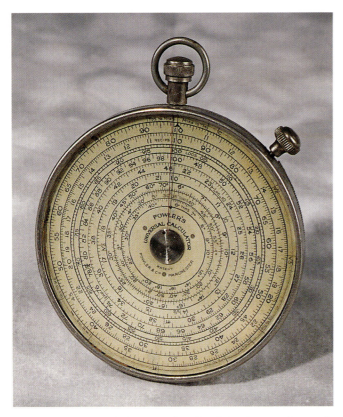

Fowler's Universal Calculator. Circular slide rule manufactured by Fowler & Company of Manchester, England. Diameter: 3.8750". Availability: Common. Value: $150.

Fowler's Calculator. Manufactured by Fowler & Company of Manchester, England. Diameter: 2.5". Availability: Common. Value: $150.

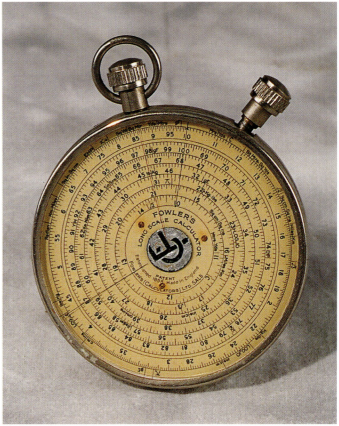

Fowler's Long Scale Calculator. Manufactured by Fowler's (calculator) LTD Sale of Manchester, England. Established 1898. Diameter: 2.5". Availability: Scarce. Value: $250.

Fowler's Textile Calculator. Manufactured by Fowler & Company of Manchester, England. Short scale-type with aluminum case. Availability: Scarce. Value: $250.

Gilson Slide Rule. Manufactured by the Gilson Slide Rule Company of Niles Michigan. Patented January 17, 1922. Copyright 1919. Dimensions: 3.7850" diameter. Availability: Common. Value: $150.

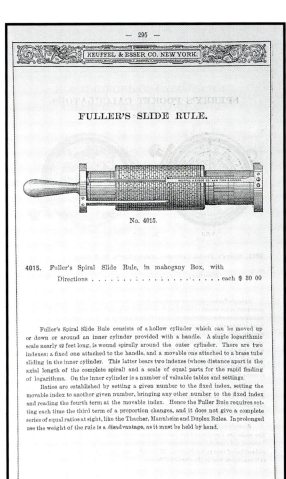

Fuller Spiral Slide Rule (Type 1). An English cylindrical slide rule manufactured by the W. F. Stanley & Company. Serial number: 3,651. First patented in 1878. A varnished cylinder measuring 17.25" long with a spiral logarithmic scale, equivalent to almost 42 feet long. Originally came in a rectangular mahogany case on which the device could be mounted on top for desktop use. The cylinder also had a handle for ease of portability. Availability: Scarce. Value: $700.

Left and above:
Halden Calculex Calculator. Circular slide rule manufactured by J. Halden & Company LTD. of Manchester, London, Newcastle, Birmingham, Leeds, and Glasgow. The first instrument is 2.3750" in diameter. It is packaged with a micro instruction manual 2.1875" x 2.8750." The second unit is housed in a nickel case. Availability: Scarce. Value: $225.

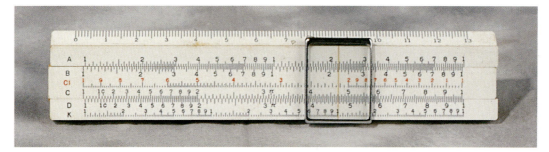

Lafayette 5" Pocket Slide Rule (Model 99-70302). Manufactured by the Lafayette Radio Electronics Corporation at 111 Jericho Turnpike in Syosset, Long Island, New York 11791. Made of bamboo. Availability: Common. Value: $10.

LePaute. A French adding device with nine place settings of clock-like dials graduated up to nineteen on each side. Both sides are beveled glass and it is mounted on a brass base. A stylus is used around the side of the device to set the mechanism. Diameter: 2.5." Availability: Scarce. Value: $300.

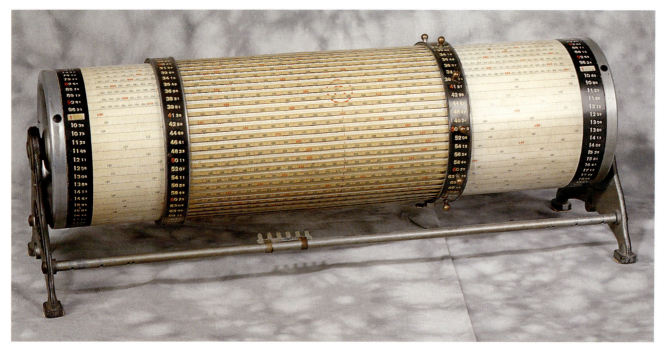

LOGA. A German slide rule of the Thatcher variety. (c.1920) Availability: Scarce. Value: $300.

Nester Slide Rule (Model 0/30). Availability: Common. Value: $45.

Otis Kings Pocket Calculator. Circular slide rule from England. Manufactured by Carbic Limited at 54 Dundanald Road of London S.W. 19. Copyright Scale No. 423. Serial Number: R969. Availability: Common. Value: $50.

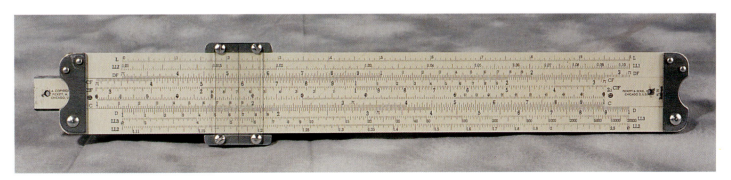

Ortho-Phase Log Log Slide Rule (Model 500). Manufactured by Pickett & Eckel, Inc. of Alhambra, California and Chicago, Illinois. Copyright 1948 with box and instructions. Availability: Common. Value: $55.

Palmers Computing Scale. An American circular slide rule dated 1843. Used for loan repayment computations and geometric calculations. It is constructed of heavy cardboard. Availability: Rare. Value: $800.

Pickett Educational Training Slide Rule (Model N1010-ES Trig.). Used in classrooms for teaching. Dimensions: 4 feet x 7.6250 inches long. Availability: Scarce. Value: $125.

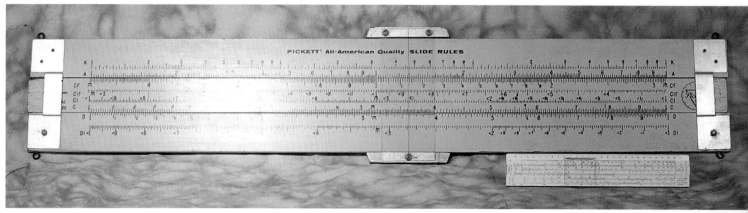

Pickett Circular Slide Rule (Model 101C). Manufactured by Pickett Industries of Santa Barbara, California. The Pickett is in its original wrapping and has never been used. It is metal and has front scales: C, C1, A, A; F, LL[1], LL[2], DS, DT; back scales: C, S, ST, T decimal equivalents. Availability: Common. Value: $20.

Post Slide Rule Display. Manufactured by Frederick Post Company of Hemmi, Japan. There are eight slides rules in the display: 4" number 1441; 5" number 1555K; 5" number 1461 (Versalog); 8" number 1445 (Student Rule); 10" number 1447 (Student Rule); 10" number 1452W (Universal Rule); Versalog number 1450F and Versalog number 1460L.

Sperry 193

Remington Rand Slide Rule (Model Fire Hazard). Made by Remington Rand, Inc. (Systems Division) and designed to factor variables such as type of building, number of floors, and intensifiers to determine the degree of record protection required. For example: does a customer need 1, 2, or 4-hour fire protection for his valuable records or documents. (c.1950) Availability: Scarce. Value: $55.

Small (Model 1). The Small Model 1 Pocket Calculator is really a slide rule that was manufactured by G. Small Company of Boston, Massachusetts. Patent date: February 12, 1918. A cylindrical device that resembles a small tape measure, with scales on the top, bottom, and sides. It measures 2" in diameter. Availability: Rare. Value: $500.

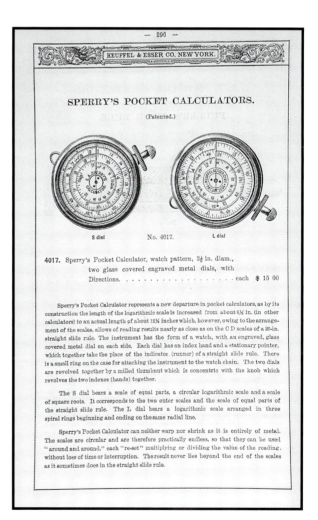

Sperry Pocket Calculator. This is an advertisement from the 1913 Keuffel & Esser catalog of the Sperry circular slide rule. Patent date: October 25, 1904. Slide rule availability: Rare. Value: $850.

Thatcher Slide Rule (Model 3147). Cylindrical slide rule invented by Edwin Thatcher in 1881. Manufactured by the Keuffel and Esser Company of Hoboken, New Jersey. This device was 18" long and 4" in diameter and was capable of results carried out to the fourth and fifth place. Problems in multiplication, division, proportion and roots involving up to three quantities are solved in one operation. Availability: Scarce. Value: $1,800.

Opposite page, bottom:
Unknown Slide Rule / Calculator. Is believed to be a slide rule device capable of performing "co-multiplication," a term used to describe the process of extending slide rule readings. The first three figures are taken from the slide rule and the co-multiplier will give as many additional figures as are desired. Availability: Scarce. Value: $300.

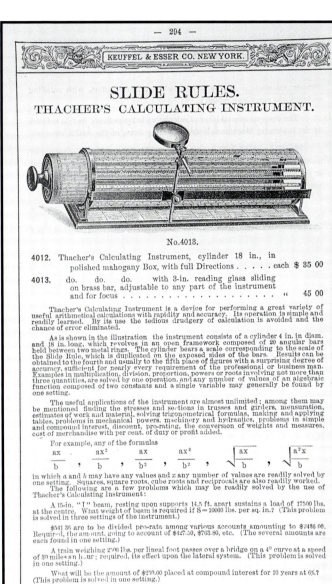

— 294 —

KEUFFEL & ESSER CO. NEW YORK.

SLIDE RULES.
THACHER'S CALCULATING INSTRUMENT.

No. 4013.

4012.	Thacher's Calculating Instrument, cylinder 18 in., in polished mahogany Box, with full Directions . . . . . each	$ 35 00
4013.	do. do. do. with 3-in. reading glass sliding on brass bar, adjustable to any part of the instrument and for focus . . . . "	45 00

Thacher's Calculating Instrument is a device for performing a great variety of useful arithmetical calculations with rapidity and accuracy. Its operation is simple and readily learned. By its use the tedious drudgery of calculation is avoided and the chance of error eliminated.

As is shown in the illustration the instrument consists of a cylinder 4 in. in diam. and 18 in. long, which revolves in an open framework composed of 20 angular bars held between two metal rings. The cylinder bears a scale corresponding to the scale of the Slide Rule, which is duplicated on the exposed sides of the bars. Results can be obtained to the fourth and usually to the fifth place of figures with a surprising degree of accuracy, sufficient for nearly every requirement of the professional or business man. Examples in multiplication, division, proportion, powers or roots involving not more than three quantities, are solved by one operation, and any number of values of an algebraic function composed of two constants and a single variable may generally be found by one setting.

The useful applications of the instrument are almost unlimited; among them may be mentioned finding the stresses and sections in trusses and girders, mensuration, estimates of work and material, solving trigonometrical formulas, making and applying tables, problems in mechanical powers, machinery and hydraulics, problems in simple and compound interest, discount, pro-rating, the conversion of weights and measures, cost of merchandise with per cent. of duty or profit added.

For example, any of the formulas

$$\frac{ax}{b}, \frac{ax^2}{b}, \frac{ax}{b^2}, \frac{ax^2}{b^2}, \sqrt{\frac{ax}{b}}, \sqrt{\frac{a^2x}{b}}$$

in which a and b may have any values and x any number of values are readily solved by one setting. Squares, square roots, cube roots and reciprocals are also readily worked.

The following are a few problems which may be readily solved by the use of Thacher's Calculating Instrument:

A 15-in. "I" beam, resting upon supports 14.5 ft. apart sustains a load of 17500 lbs. at the centre. What weight of beam is required if S = 10000 lbs. per sq. in.? (This problem is solved in three settings of the instrument.)

$541.36 are to be divided pro-rata among various accounts amounting to $7486.00. Required, the amount going to account of $427.50, $763.80, etc. (The several amounts are each found in one setting.)

A train weighing 2500 lbs. per lineal foot passes over a bridge on a 4° curve at a speed of 30 miles an hour; required, its effect upon the lateral system. (This problem is solved in one setting.)

What will be the amount of $250.00 placed at compound interest for 10 years at 6%? (This problem is solved in one setting.)

Wichmann. A circular slide rule manufactured by the Wichmann Company of Germany. Diameter: 2.5." Availability: Scarce. Value: $250.

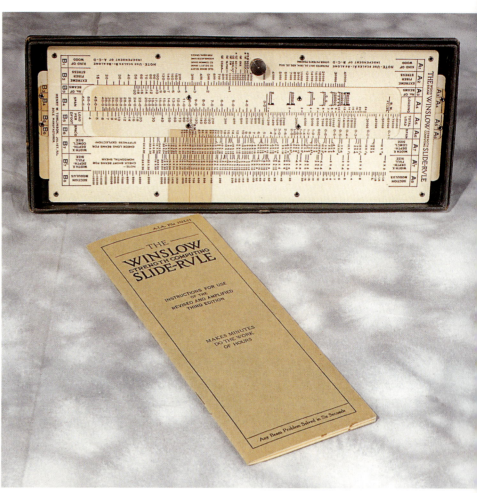

Winslow Slide Rule. Manufactured by Henry W. Tomlinson of Joliet, Illinois. Invented by Benjamin E. Winslow. This slide rule computes the structural strength of steel beams. Availability: Scarce. Value: $75.

In answer to the question, "Whatever happened to slide rules?" perhaps this advertisement by IBM in the 1950s tells the story. The new IBM electronic calculator is like having 150 extra engineers with slide rules. But, it wasn't the big IBM calculator that replaced slide rules, it was the small pocket electronic calculators that emerged in the 1970s and are discussed in the next chapter.

Chapter Six
Electronic Calculators and Desktop Computers

Charles Babbage (1791-1871) was the first person to conceive the idea of and draw the plans for a general-purpose programmable computing machine (c.1834). It was to be an all-mechanical device that could add, subtract, multiply, and divide in any sequence. It would have *store* and *mill* capabilities (equal to modern computers) and *memory* and *processing*. It could also be programmed using a punch card system that Babbage borrowed from the Jacquard loom of 1804. Babbage even designed a printing device for this "computer."

The only problem was that Babbage's ideas were far ahead of the capabilities of the mechanical technology of his time. Without government support, he gave up his project, but he left a full set of plans and his notes. In 1979, approximately 150 years later, the Curator of Computing at the University of Sydney, Australia, developed a proposal to build a working model using Babbage's notes, drawings, and plans.

Six more years passed, then Doran D. Swade, an electronics engineer and the Senior Curator of the Computing and Control Section of the Science Museum of London, England, accepted the challenge. In 1985, Swade and his associates began to build "Babbage's Difference Engine." The project was successfully completed nine years later, in 1991. From the date of conception to completion, almost 160 years had elapsed.

Now the world would no longer hypothesize that Babbage might have created the first mechanical computer. Swade and his associates had proved once and for all that a mathematician in 1834 had the creative foresight to design the world's first computer. One can only speculate the advancement that could have been achieved had Babbage completed his invention.

By 1958, the time was ripe for a breakthrough in mechanical calculators. The calculator industry had become a replacement market many years before. Some manufacturers sold the same basic model for over ten years. Cosmetic changes in appearance were often considered the innovation of the day.

In 1958, the British manufacturer, Bell Punch Company, Ltd., patented the world's first electronic desktop calculator. Patent number 868,753-19656/58. It was first placed on the market in 1963. The British company, Bell Punch, called their new product the "Anita." It used "transistor technology."

A few years later, across the ocean, an American company, Texas Instruments, announced another breakthrough in the calculator industry. A team of Texas Instruments engineers had developed an "integrated circuit" chip. In the early 1970s Texas Instruments along with several other manufacturers began mass-producing "pocket electronic calculators."

Electronic Calculators

Anita. Manufactured by the Bell Punch Co., Ltd. of London, England. The manufacturer advertised it as "The World's First Electronic Calculator." It was first patented in Great Britain in 1958 (Patent number 868,753-19656/58), and placed on the market in 1963. At present the Anita is considered very collectible. Dimensions: 15" w x 17.50" d x 10.25" h. Availability: Scarce. Value: $400.

Right:
Bomar Scientific Calculator (Model MX 100). Manufactured by Bowmar/ALI, 531 Main Street of Acton, Massachusetts. The Bowmar was a palm-size mid-1970s electronic calculator capable of scientific functions. Serial number: 101,362. Availability: Scarce. Value: $35.

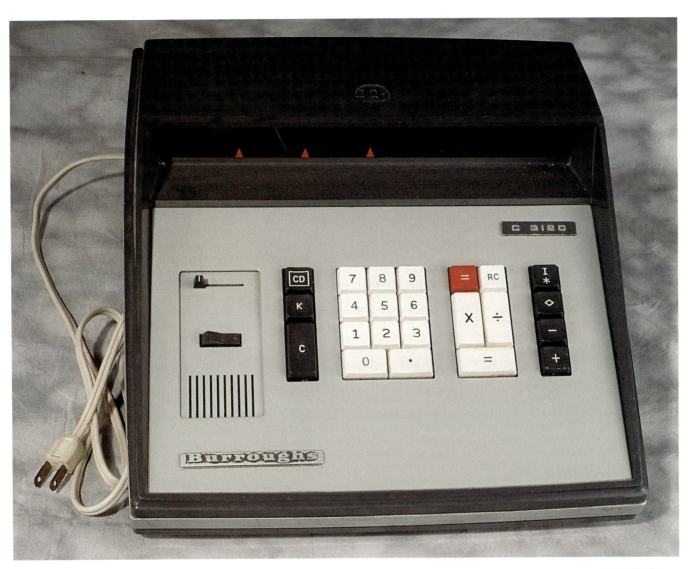

Burroughs (Model C3120). A desktop electronic calculator made in Japan. Serial number: C-27,964J. Availability: Common. Value: $25.

Right:
Casio (Model FX-10). A scientific hand-held electronic calculator. Serial number: 8,055,232. Availability: Common. Value: $20.

Hewlett Packard Scientific (Model HP-25). Electronic hand-held calculator. Made in Singapore. (c.1975) Serial number: 1804S25,699. Availability: Scarce. Value: $20.

Hewlett Packard (Model HP-35). Electronic hand-held calculator. This was Hewlett Packard's first electronic calculator and was introduced in 1972. It was manufactured in the United States. Serial number: 1230A93,517. Availability: Scarce. Value: $200.

Hewlett Packard (Model HP-65 Programmable). Electronic hand-held scientific calculator. This was one of the first programmable calculators that used magnetic cards for storage. (c.1974) Serial number: 1511A01955. Availability: Scarce. Value: $125.

Panasonic 201

Hewlett Packard (Model HP-71B Programmable). One of the early electronic laptop computers that was programmable in "Basic." It has a liquid crystal display of 22 characters, a "qwerty" typewriter keyboard and a ten-key touch pad for rapid numerical entry. (c.1984) Availability: Scarce. Value: $50.

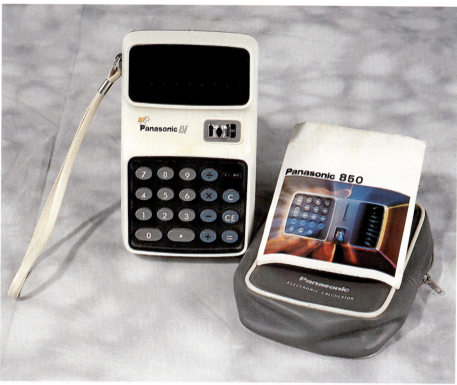

Panasonic (Model JE850U). Availability: Scarce. Value: $50.

National Semi-Conductor (Model Novus 4520). This electronic calculator was also called the "Scientist." It was a full-featured scientific model that appeared about 1977. Serial number: 117,227. Availability: Common. Value: $15.

Remington, Remington Rand, and Sperry Rand

In 1966, Remington Rand entered the electronic desk calculator market with a product called the EDC III. An EDC I and ID followed in rapid order. The following examples show the Remington electronic desk and hand-held calculator products. It was during this period that the Remington calculator became a consumer product. This meant that it was no longer economical to send direct salesmen out to sell the product. As a consumer product, the calculator would be sold through retail chains, direct mail, etc. Availability: Scarce. Value: $50.

Sperry Rand (Model EDC 1D). Serial number: D57,489. Availability: Scarce. Value: $175.

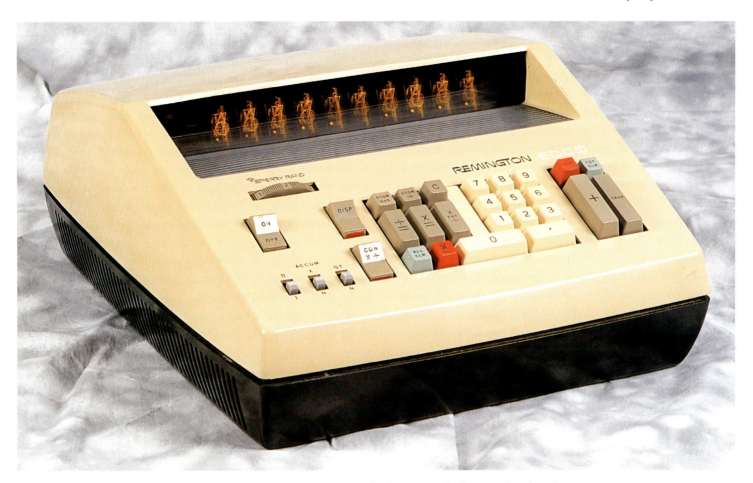

Sperry Rand (Model EDC III). This was the first model of Remington's electronic calculator product line. It made its first appearance on the market in 1966. The first models used "nixie tubes" for the display. Serial number: 38,281. Availability: Scarce.
Value: $150.

Sperry Rand (Model EDC 1603). This was a late 1960s "nixie tube" electronic calculator by Remington Rand. It was the last of the larger desktop electronics by Remington. Serial number: 306,594. Availability: Scarce.
Value: $135.

204 Sperry Rand

Sperry Rand (Model 661 D Palm Size). Remington hand-held electronic calculator. Serial number: 968,743. Availability: Common. Value: $25.

Sperry Rand (Model 665 Palm Size). Remington hand-held electronic calculator. Serial number: 7,121,747. Availability: Common. Value: $25.

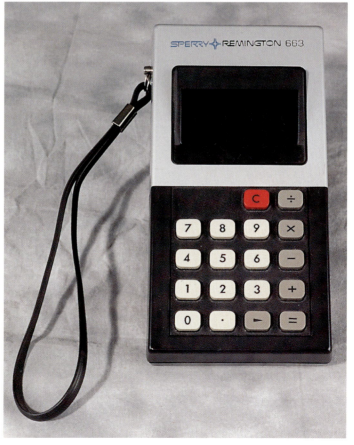

Sperry Rand (Model 663 Palm Size). Remington hand-held electronic calculator. Serial number: 2,138,286. Availability: Common. Value: $25.

Sperry Rand 205

Sperry Rand (Model 801B Palm Size). Remington electronic calculator. Serial number: B807,085. Availability: Common. Value: $25.

Sperry Rand (Model 803B Portable). Remington electronic portable calculator. Serial number: 910,381. Availability: Common. Value: $25.

Sperry Rand

Sperry Rand (Model 807B Portable). Remington electronic calculator. Serial number: 136,365. Availability: Common. Value: $25.

Sperry Rand (Model 819). Square root and percentage. Serial number: 29,036,148. Availability: Scarce. Value: $50.

Sperry Rand (Model 809SR). This was Remington's square root model and was made in Japan. Serial number: 2,112,142. Availability: Scarce. Value: $45.

Sperry Rand (Model 821 GT Portable). Remington electronic calculator with grand total feature. Serial number: 2,101,380. Availability: Common. Value: $25.

Sperry Rand (Model 1005 B). Remington electronic calculator. Serial number: 2,101,896. Availability: Scarce. Value: $125.

Sperry Rand (Model 823 GT Portable). Remington electronic calculator with grand total feature. Serial number: 2,110,723. Availability: Common. Value: $25.

208   Sperry Rand

Sperry Rand (Model 1201GT Lektronic). Remington electronic calculator, desk size with grand total. Serial number: 313,326. Availability: Scarce. Value: $50.

Sperry Rand (Model 1213). Remington electronic calculator, desk size. Serial number: B830,094. Availability: Common. Value: $35.

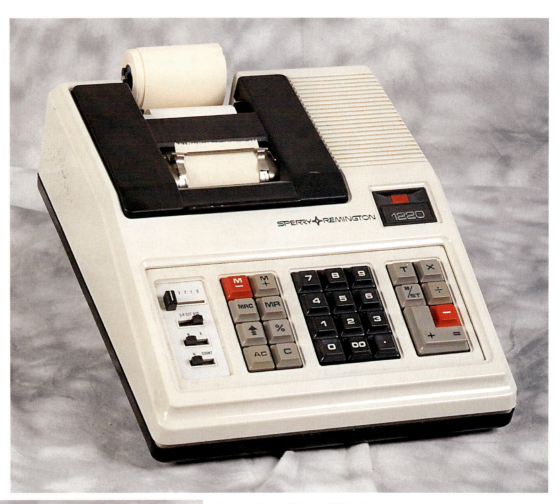

Sperry Rand (Model 1220). Remington electronic calculator, desk size. Serial number: C3,307,508. Availability: Scarce. Value: $125.

Sperry Rand (Model SSR-8). This was Remington's scientific version of the hand-held electronic calculator. Serial number: 26,056,284. Availability: Scarce. Value: $55.

210 Sharp

Sharp Elsi-Mate (Model EL-8016R). Electronic hand-held calculator with four function capability. Serial number: 62,164,673. Availability: Common. Value: $10.

Texas Instruments (Model SR40). Hand-held electronic scientific calculator. (c.1973) Serial number: 3,201,291. Patent number: 3,924,110. Availability: Common. Value: $35.

Sinclair Electronic (Gold) Availability: Scarce. Value: $225.

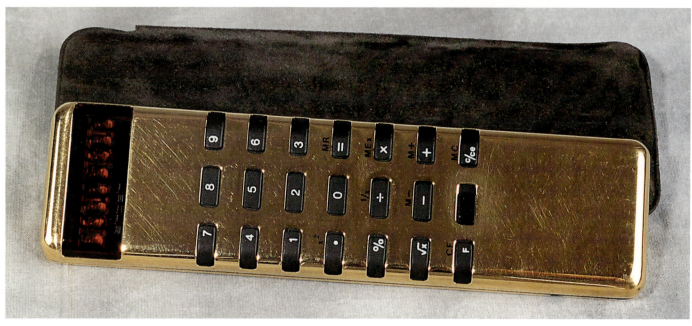

Texas Instruments (Model 2500 Datamath). This was Texas Instruments' first hand-held calculator that appeared in 1972. Included the original box, instruction manual, adapter/charger, and leather carrying case. Serial number: 286,303 Availability: Rare. Value: $200.

Victor (Model MEC 225). Manufactured by the Victor Comptometer Corporation, Business Products Group of Chicago, Illinois. Serial number: 5164-107. (c.1971) Availability: Scarce: Value: $75.

Apple IIc

Desktop Computers

The January 1975 issue of *Popular Electronics Magazine*, featured an article on how to build a small desktop computer. A kit was available and for approximately $350 you could build your own. It was called the "Altair 8800" microprocessor and it used a cassette for storage. Its black box appearance wasn't much to look at, but most experts agree that it was the beginning of the desktop computer market.

Two years later, Steve Jobs and Steve Wozniak formed a company called Apple Computer and introduced the "Apple II", a personal computer so popular that over two million systems were sold.

It was not until 1981 that IBM announced their first microcomputer and called it simply the IBM PC model 5150. Its operating system was called "MS-DOS" or Micro Soft Disk Operating System. So began the endless list of "clone" manufacturers and spawned an industry with revenues climbing to $115 million by 1988.

Desktop computers do not truly qualify as "antiques" since the earliest models only go back 25 years. But the nostalgia and interest of all of us who watched this wonderful "technology revolution" has made these early industry relics highly collectible with values that will increase exponentially.

Apple IIc MicroComputer (Enhanced). Manufactured by the Apple Computer Company of Cupertino, California. Patent numbers are 4,278,972; 4,136,359 and 4,130,862. Serial number: 252D5411LBA25-2064. The operating system was called ProDOS. Availability: Common. Value: $150.

Commodore (VIC 20). Manufactured by Commodore Business Machines and made in Taiwan. Serial number: 640,027 and includes a cassette drive and software for Inventory and Personal Finance 1 & 2. (c.1980) Availability: Common. Value: $75.

LISA Micro Computer (Model A6650300KB). Manufactured by Apple Computer Company of Cupertino, California. LISA was an acronym for "local integrated software architecture." This machine was the beginning of the Apple Macintosh product line, which was very popular due to its "user friendly" software. By using a combined system of graphic and menu architecture, the computer was easy to use. Serial number: 1,030,187. (c.1983) Availability: Scarce. Value: $1,000.

Osborne Portable Computer (Model OCC1). Manufactured by the Osborne Computer Corporation, of Hayward, California. This was the first portable computer to appear (c.1981) and it weighed only 23 pounds. It ran on a CP/M operating system and had two built in 5.25" floppy disk drives. Serial number: 234,351. Availability: Scarce. Value: $400.

Below and right:
Otrona Portable Computer (Model Attaché). Manufactured by Otrona Advanced System Corporation of Boulder, Colorado. A CP/M based system introduced in 1982. Availability: Scarce. Value: $300.

216 Otrona

Otrona Portable Computer (Model 2001). Manufactured by the Otrona Advanced System Corporation at 4725 Walnut Street in Boulder, Colorado. Serial number: 43,064. (c.1983) Availability: Scarce. Value: $150.

Radio Shack, TRS-80 MicroComputer (Model III). Manufactured by Radio Shack, a division of the Tandy Corporation of Fort Worth, Texas. Serial number: 107,526. (c.1980) Availability: Common. Value: $75.

Texas Instruments (Model 99/4A) – Manufactured by Texas Instruments Corporation. Patent number: 3,757,306. (c.1979) Availability: Common. Value: $74.

Victor Micro Computer (Model 9000). Manufactured by Victor Comptometer, a division of the Kidde Company. The Victor 9000 was a CP/M based system. When IBM announced that their new operating system would be MS/DOS, Victor became one of the fatalities in the industry. Also pictured is a full-page newspaper advertisement of the Victor 9000. Serial number: 33,291. (c.1982) Availability: Scarce. Value: $200.

Victor's Desktop Business Computer System.

Businesses today face a basic dilemma when it comes to selecting a computer.

So-called "personal" computers have limited power and capacity. They're just too small to be useful to most businesses.

And the larger mini computers are more expensive.

Victor has a solution to that dilemma.

The Victor 9000 Business Computer is priced under $5,000. Like a "personal."

Yet the Victor 9000 has a capacity that rivals the expensive minis.

A close look at the chart on the right shows you just how the Victor 9000 compares.

The Victor gives you the kind of memory and storage capacity business applications demand. Much more than the IBM Personal Computer, the Apple III or their competitors.

And the Victor display screen has double the resolution and capacity of its competitors. It can display a full 132-column report and still be perfectly readable. Is that important to your business? Ask your accountant.

The Victor display monitor also swivels to the left and right and tilts forward and backward for optimum viewing ease. The keyboard is free-standing and can be placed for maximum comfort and convenience.

Experience where it counts.

But the chart shows you only the obvious advantages of the Victor 9000. It doesn't show Victor's 65 years of experience in solving business application problems. And it doesn't show Victor's 50 branch offices and hundreds of dealers strategically located throughout the country providing fast service and total support. It's most assuring to know that Victor will be just a phone call away as long as you own your Victor 9000.

A software library that keeps on growing.

Victor offers a library of tested and proven business software, from accounting to word processing. And we're committed to continual development of wide-ranging business application software.

There's also a complete line of peripherals and accessories available for the 9000.

Mini power, micro price and Victor support. That's an unbeatable combination. And it's produced a desktop computer system that's easy to use and designed to make your business more efficient and profitable. It's the Victor 9000. And it's ready for delivery today.

Change the way you solve business problems. Get in touch with Victor at (800) 621-5559. In Illinois (800) 972-5858. We're open 24 hours a day, 7 days a week.

VICTOR BUSINESS PRODUCTS
Subsidiary of Kidde, Inc.
KIDDE

MAKE & MODEL	Victor 9000	IBM PC	Xerox 820	Apple III	Radio Shack TRS80 Model II
Processor Type	8088	8088	Z80A	6502	Z80A
Word Length	16 bits	16 bits	8 bits	8 bits	8 bits
Memory Size (Internal)	128-896KB	16-256KB	64KB	96-256KB	32-64KB
Storage Capacity on 2 Floppies	2400KB (5¼")	640KB (5¼")	184KB (5¼")	280KB (5¼")	960KB (8")
CRT Display Standard Format	80 x 25	80 x 25	80 x 24	80 x 24	80 x 24
Alternate Format	132 x 50	None	None	None	None
Graphics Resolution	800 x 400	640 x 200	None	560 x 192	None
Communications Built-in Serial Ports at no extra cost	2	0	2	1	2
Built-in Parallel Ports at no extra cost	1	0	2	0	1
Human Factors Keys on Keyboards	94-104	83	96	74	76
Detached Keyboard	Yes	Yes	Yes	No	Yes
Tilting Display mechanism	Yes	No	No	No	No
Swivelling Display mechanism	Yes	No	No	No	No
Desk Area Required (Approx. Square In. with 2 floppy disks)	310	420	470	361	500
Operating System Supplied Standard	CP/M-86 MS-DOS	None	None	Apple DOS	TRS DOS

NOTE: Chart based on manufacturer's information and Dataquest, Inc. available as of April 4, 1982.

You're invited to an open house.

See the exciting new Victor 9000 desktop business computer and the Victor Vanguard cash register systems at a special open house showing.

The Dates: Tuesday, June 15 and Wednesday, June 16

The Time: 9 am to 5 pm

The Place: The Delaware Suite, Hotel DuPont, 11th and Market Sts., Wilmington, Delaware.

Refreshments will be served.

If you can join us, please RSVP by calling Delaware Office Equipment (302) 478-7500. If you cannot join us, please call Delaware Office Equipment (302) 478-7500 for a special appointment. We're located at 3302 Concord Pike, Wilmington, Delaware 19803.

VICTOR®

Serving American business for 65 years.

Authorized Victor Dealer: Delaware Office Equipment, 3302 Concord Pike, Wilmington, Delaware 19803   (302) 478-7500.

Chapter Seven
Time Line

Year	Calculating Devices	Computing Technology	Historic Events
14th Century			
1300	• Abacus-Chinese		•Escapement Clock
1337			•100 Year War begins
1347			•Rats spread Bubonic Plague
1350			•Hand cannon is developed in Europe
15th Century			
1405			•Wood screw invented in Germany
1421			•Italy starts procedure issuing patents to inventors
1450			•Gutenberg Press
1492			•Columbus sails the "Ocean Blue"
16th Century			
1500			•Renaissance period begins •Gunpowder used in weapons
1503			•Leonardo DiVinci begins to paint the "Mona Lisa"
1543			•Nicolaus Copernicus book "Revolutions of the Heavenly Sphere" is printed – stating that the planets revolve around the sun
1560			•Pencil developed
1590			•Compound Microscope •William Shakespeare begins to write his first play
1592			•Galileo – Thermometer
17th Century			
1600	• Abacus-Japanese • Abacus-Russian		
1615			•British begin to drink tea
1616			•Copernicus' book is banned by the Roman Catholic Church
1617	• Napier, John "Rabbdologia," "Napiers Bones"		
1620			•Mayflower lands at Plymouth Rock
1622	• Oughtred Circular Slide Rule		
1623	• Schickard, Wm. drawing of mechanical calculator		
1642	• Pascal, Blaise first mechanical adding machine		
1660			•German flintlock pistol
1661			•Bank notes begin to be used
1667			•First blood transfusion
1673			•Hugens pendulum clock
1674	• Leibniz, Wilhelm Gottfried – stepped drum mechanism for calculators		

Year	Calculating Devices	Computing Technology	Historic Events
1682			•Halley sights comet and predicts its return
18th Century			
1704			•Graham makes the Orrery
1718			•First machine gun
1731			•Octant by Hadley and Godfrey
1742			•Centrigrade temperature
1752			•International dateline shifts America one day forward •Lightning rod
1757			•Sextant developed
1765			•Watts "Perfected Steam Engine" appears
1773			•Boston Tea Party
1776			•Jefferson drafts the "Declaration of Independence" •George Washington becomes "Commander of the Continental Army"
1779			•Boer War begins
1783			•Parachute invented
1784			•Bifocals
1789			•Guillotine invented
1791			•Metric system begins
1795			•Harrison develops Chronometer
1798			•Lithograph
1799			•Rosetta Stone discovered
19th Century			
1800			•Volta battery
1803			•U.S.A. makes the Louisiana Purchase •Railroad locomotive
1804			•Jacquard, Joseph Marie designed punch card to weave a pattern •Napoleon Boneparte crowns himself as Emperor
1807			•Gas street lighting begins
1812			•War of 1812 begins
1816			•Stethoscope appears
1817			•Erie Canal construction starts
1820	• Thomas deColmar Arithmometer		
1821			•Faraday's electric motor •Napoleon Boneparte dies on the Island of St. Helena
1822	• Babbage begins construction of difference engine		•Irish Potato Famine

Year	Calculating Devices	Computing Technology	Historic Events
1829			• Stephenson's locomotive
1834	• Babbage details plan for an analytical engine		
1835			• Texas revolution
1837			• Telegraph
1839			• Bicycle
1842	• Chesterman Slide Rule		
1843	• Palmer Slide Rule		
1844			• Morse Code is developed
1845	• Leavitt Calculator		
1847			• California Gold Rush
1853			• First glider • Hypodermic Syringe
1854	• Hatfield Adder		• Kerosene • Vacuum tube invented • Crimean War begins
1855			• Printing telegraph
1856			• Nitroglycerine
1857			• Murray begins to work on the *Oxford English Dictionary* • New York Stock Market Panic
1858		• Punched paper tape developed	
1861			• First color photograph • First postcard • Start of the Civil War
1862			• Pasteur invents "pasteurization" • Abraham Lincoln's "Emancipation Proclamation"
1864			• Start of the Red Cross
1865			• Dynamite developed
1867			• Barbed wire created • Diamonds discovered in Africa
1868	• Webb		
1869			• Suez Canal opened • Start of the Women's Suffrage League
1870	• Groesbeck Calc.		
1873			• Christopher Latham Sholes Typewriter
1874	• Original Odhner Calculator		
1875	• Adder, The (Webb) Baldwin Calc.		• First mimeograph –Thomas A. Edison • Mark Twain writes "Tom Sawyer"
1876			• Bell's telephone
1878	• Bill Adder • Burkhardt • Arithmometer • Fuller Slide Rule		
1879	• Hart Adder		• First Cash Register –James Ritty
1881	• Thatcher Slide Rule		• First Dictation machine – Bell
1882			• First electric lights
1883			• Brooklyn Bridge is finished
1884	• Spalding Calculator		• Fountain Pen is developed
1885	• Burroughs, John Seward files for adding machine patent		• Mergenthaler invents the Linotype
1886	• Felt, Dorr E invents the Comptometer		• Coca-Cola begins • Statue of Liberty – a gift from France
1888			• First motion picture
1889	• Comptograph		
1890		• Hollerinth invents the tabulating machine for Census Bureau	• USA established

Year	Calculating Devices	Computing Technology	Historic Events
1892	• Universal Adder		• First Diesel engine –named after the inventor
1893	• Millionaire • Rapid		• Automatic pistol
1895	• Lightning (Cardboard) Adder • Saxonia Arithmometer		
1896			• Start of the modern day Olympics
1897	• Remington introduces first vertical acctg. machine	• Thompson discovers the electron	• Cathode Ray Tube • Aspirin appears
1898			• Benz automobile starts • War between US and Spain • Start of the Boxer Rebellion

20th Century

Year	Calculating Devices	Computing Technology	Historic Events
1900	• Charpentier • Calculimétre Slide Rule • Herring, J. L. • Mechanical Accountant • Stephenson		• Movies begin to talk
1901	• Locke Adder		
1902	• Dalton Adding Machine		
1903	• Adix Adder • Standard (Model B) • Wales Adding Machine		• Wright Brothers take to the air
1904	• Automatic – Golden Gem • Gancher • Peerless • Triumphator		• Panama Canal contruction begins
1905	• Bri-Cal • Computator • Mercedes-Euklid Calc.		• Einstein publishes "Theory of Relativity"
1906	• Achimedes Calc. • Arithstyle Adder • Ellis – Accounting Machine		
1907	• Ensign Calc. • Remington Vertical Accounting Machine • The first adding & subtrating typewriter • TIM Calc.		
1908	• Lightning Adder • Madas Calc. • Pangborn Calc. • Wahl		
1909	• Calculus Calc. • Comptator		• Admiral Peary reaches the North Pole
1910	• Barrett • Elliott Fisher • Midget • Triumph • Underwood Bookkeeping		• Woodrow Wilson becomes President
1911	• Bassett • Marchant • Monroe		
1912	• Austin • Moon Hopkins		
1913	• American • Argos • Baum, Michael • Federal		
1914	• Sundstrand		• Model T Ford • World War I begins • First traffic light in England
1915	• Commonwealth • Denominator		
1916			• Tank invented
1917			• US enters WW I
1918	• Facit • Small Slide Rule • Victor		• WW I ends
1919	• Automatic (Laughlin)		

Year	Calculating Devices	Computing Technology	Historic Events
1920	• Allen, R. C. • Bug • Consul – The Educated Monkey		•Hitler forms Nazi Party
1921	• Arrow • Summator		
1922	• Add-Index • Amco • Britannic		•King Tut's Tomb is found by Howard Carter
1923	• Portable • Rapid (pinwheel)		
1924	• Atlas Slide • Rheinmetall		
1925	• Hamann-Manus		
1926	• Addac		
1927			•Charles Lindbergh's flight to France
1928	• Adding Machine		
1929			•Stock Market Crash
1934			•Nylon stockings
1936		•Turring, Allen describes computer concept	•First Helicopter
1937	• Add-O-Matic		
1938		•Zuse, Conrad completes Z-1 computer in his parents' living room	
1939			•WW II begins
1941			•Japanese attack on Pearl Harbor
1943		•English built "Collossius" cracks German secret code	
1945			•Atomic Bomb dropped •WW II ends
1946		•"Eniac" – first programmable electronic digital computer	
1947		•Bell Laboratories announces its transistor	
1950	• Curta	•Eckert-Mauchly Computer Corp sold to Remington Rand	•Safety matches appear •First credit card "Diner's Club"
1952		•"Univac," first commercial computer delivered to U.S. Census Bureau	•DNA discovered by Crick & Watson
1955			•Vietnam War begins
1956			•Elvis Presley appears on the scene
1957	• Addo-X		
1958		•First integrated circuit by American, Jack Kirby of Texas Instruments and Robert Noyse of Fairchild Semi-Conductor	•Jet airline passenger service begins in US •Townes invents laser •Alaska becomes 49th state
1960		•First Modem by Dataphone	
1963	• Fowler Slide Rule	•Computer revenues total "1 billion dollars"	
1968		•First "mouse" by Douglas Ingebart	
1969			•Neil Armstrong walks on the Moon
1970		•Floppy Disk	
1971		•First Micro-Processor •First 8" Floppy-Alan Shugart	
1972		•First hand-held scientific calculator HP-35	
1975		•First "Do-It-Yourself" computer – Altair 8800	
1976			•Viking I lands on Mars
1977		•First Micro-computer – Apple II - invented by Jobs and Wosniak	
1978		•PC computer	
1979		•First "spreadsheet" "Visacalc"	•Sony Walkman
1981		•First portable computer - "Osborne I"	
1984		•First "User Friendly" computer – Apple McIntosh	

21ST Century

Year	Calculating Devices	Computing Technology	Historic Events
2000			•World Population reaches 6 billion •Closest Presidential election in American history

Bibliography

Cargil, G. Knott. *Transactions of the Asiatic Society of Japan, The Abacus.* Tokyo, Japan: University of Tokyo, 1886.
Durant, W. N. *Counting Machines Catalog.* Milwaukee, Wisconsin: Durant Manufacturing Company, 1915.
Durant, Will. *Our Oriental Heritage, The Story of Civilization.* Norwalk, Connecticut: The Easton Press, 1992.
Fisher, Harrison. *Business Machines.* Chicago, Illinois: American Technical Society, 1959.
Haddock, Thomas F. *A Collectors Guide to Personal Computers and Pocket Calculators.* Florence, Alabama: Books of America, Inc. 1993.
Halacy, Dan. *Charles Babbage, Father of the Computer.* New York, New York: The Macmillan Company, 1980.
Hill, Henry Chase. *The Story of Calculating Machines, The Wonder Book of Knowledge.* Philadelphia, Pennsylvania: The John C. Winston Co., 1919.
Sperry Rand Corporation. *A History of Sperry Rand Corporation.* U.S.A. Recording and Statistical Division of Sperry Rand Corp., 1967.
Johnson, Alan. *Frank Stephen Baldwin.* Dictionary of American Biography. New York, New York: Charles Scribner's Sons, 1928.
Keuffel & Esser Co. *Keuffel & Esser Co. Catalog.* New York, New York: Keuffel & Esser Co., 1913.
Malone, Dumas. *C. H. Webb, Dictionary of American Biography.* New York, New York: Charles Scribner's Sons, 1953.
McCarthy, James H. *American Equipment Digest.* Chicago, Illinois: 1924.
Martin, Ernst. (translated and edited by Peggy Aldrich Kidwell and Michael R. Williams.) *Die Rechenmaschinen. Los Angeles/San Francisco, California:* Tomash Publishers, 1992.
Montgomerie, G. A. *Digital Calculating Machines.* London, Glasgow: Blackie & Son Limited, 1956.
Root, C. J., Company. *Counting Machines Catalog.* C. J. Root Co., 1915.
Smith, George. *John Napier, The Dictionary of National Biography* London, England: Oxford University Press, 1917.
Smith, George. *Charles Babbage, The Dictionary of National Biography.* London, England: Oxford University Press, 1917.
Starr, Harris C. *Wm. Seward Burroughs, The Dictionary of National Biography.* New York, New York: Charles Scribner's Sons, 1944.
Swade, Doran D. *Redeeming Charles Babbage's Mechanical Computer.* New York, New York: Scientific American, Inc., February, 1993.
Turck, J. A. V. *Origin of Modern Calculating Machines,* New York, New York: Arno Press, 1972.
Williams, Michael R. *A History of Computing Technology.* Englewood Cliffs, New Jersey: Prentice-Hall, 1985.

Index

Abacus (stchoty) 13
Abacus (swan pan) 13
Abacus (soroban) 13
Acumath 179
Addac 14
Add-A-Skill 14
Add-Em 14
Add-Index 15, 154
Adder, The 15
Adder, The (Cardboard) 15
Addiator (Addfeet Junior) 16
Addiator (Fractomator) 16
Addimult (Sumax-E) 16
Adding Machine 17
Addipresto 17
Add-O-Matic 18
Addometer 18
Addo-X 19
Adix 19
ALCO 179
Allen, R. C. 19, 20
Amco 20
American 20, 21, 149, 155, 156
Anita 11, 198
Apple 212
Archimedes 22
Argos 22
Arithma 23
Arithstyle 23
Arrow 24
Atlas 180
Austin 24
Automatic 25, 26, 27, 157 158
Automatic (Laughlin) 25
Baby 27
Bair-Fulton 28
Baldwin 29, 30
Barrett 31, 32, 33
Bassett 34
Baum, Michel 34
Bill 35
Bomar 198
Boyer's Machine Shop 39
Bri-Cal 35
Britannic 36
Brunsviga 36, 37
BUC 37
Burkhardt 38
Burroughs 39, 40, 41, 42, 43, 44, 45, 159, 171, 199

Burroughs Moon-Hopkins 173
Calculigraphe 180
Calculagraph 45, 46
Calculus 180
Calculator 47
Calcumeter 44
Cardboard Adder 48
Casio 199
Chadwick 48
Charpentier Calculimètre 181
Chart, American Digest of Business Machines 7
Chesterman 182
Clary 49
Commodore 213
Commonwealth 50
Computator 50
Comptograph 61
Comptometer 10, 62, 63, 64
Consul 51
Contex 51
Conto 51
Corexa 52
Corona 52
Counter Mechanism 148
Cray 52
Curta 53
Dactyle 54
Dalton 54, 159, 171
Darney's 55
Denominator 55
Dial-A-Matic 55
Dollad 56
Durant 148, 150
Elliott Fisher 173, 174
Ellis 56, 172
Elm City 151, 152
Ensign 56
Everest 56
Faber, A. W. 182
Faber Castell 183
Facit 56
Federal 58, 59
Feliks 59
Felt, Dorr E. 60
Felt & Tarrant 60, 61, 62, 63, 64
Fites-Peerless 64
Fowler 64, 184, 185

Friden 65
Fuller 187
Gancher 66
Gilson 186
Golden Gem 67, 68
Groesbeck 69
Halden 187
Hamann-Manus 69
Hart 69
Hasbro 70
Hatfield 70
Hercules Powder 165
Herring, J. L. 70, 72, 146
Hewlett Packard 200, 201
Hines 72
Hoffritz 71
Högfors 73
Houghton Oil 164
International 161, 162, 163, 164, 165
Itemiser 73
Kalkometer 73
Kee-Pa-Count 74
Ken + Add 74
Kes-Add 74
Keuffel & Esser 146
Key 75
Lafayette 188
Lamb 75
Leavitt 76
LePaute 188
Lightning 77, 78
Lisa 213
Locke 78
LOGA 188
MADAS 78
Magic Multiplying Pencil 79
Marbels Blood Cell 79
Marchant 79, 80, 81, 82
Master 82
McCaskey 166
Mechanical Accountant 83
Meilicke 84
Mercedes-Euklid 84
Midget 85
Millionaire 10, 86, 87
Monroe 88, 89, 90
Moon Hopkins 175
Multi-Vider 91
Napier, John 178
Napier's Bones 178
National Semi-Conductor 201

Nester 189
Nippon 91
Numeria 91
Olivetti, Camillo 92
Olivetti 92, 93
Original Odhner 94, 95
Ortho-Phase 189
Osborne 214
'O' Talley 152
Otis King 189
Otrona 215, 216
Palmer's 190
Panasonic 201
Pangborn 95
Peerless 95
Piccolo-S 96
Pickett 190, 191
Plus 97
Portable 52, 97
Post 192
Precise 98
Produx 987
Quick-Add 98
Quixsum 99
Radio Shack 217
Rand, James H. 102
Rapid 99, 100
Ray 101
Recording Lumber Measurer 29
Reischer 101
Remington 102, 103, 104, 105, 106, 107, 108, 167, 169, 176, 202
Remington Rand 193, 202
Reuter's Saxonia 109
Rheinmetall 109, 110
Root, C. J. 150, 151
Russo, Thomas A.
Saxonia 110, 111
Schickard 8, 112
Sharp 210
Silver King 152
Sinclair 210
Small 193
Smith, L. C. 146
Solo 113
Spalding 113
Sperry 193
Sperry Rand 202, 203, 204, 205, 206, 207, 208, 209
Standard 114

Starr 115
Stephenson 115
Stetson, John B. Hat Company 165
Sumaster 116
Summator 116
Sumit 116
Summax-E 16, 116
Sundstand 117, 167
Swift 118
Tasco 118
Tarema 118
Tate Arithmometer 118
Texas Instrument 211, 217
Thatcher 194, 195
Thomas de Colmar 9, 120
Tiger 121
TIM 121, 122
Time Computer 122
Tip 123
Tom Thumb 123
Torpedo 123
Totalizer 170
Tower 124
Triumph 124, 125
Type-Adder 170
Underwood 168, 177
Underwood Sundstrand 126
Unitas 127
Universal 128, 129
Unknown 129, 153, 194, 195
Valient 129
Ve-Po-Ad 130
Victor 131, 132, 133, 134, 135, 136, 211, 218
Wahl 170
Wales 137, 138, 139
Wales, Charles 58
Walther 140
Wang 140
Webb 141
Webb Types 142, 143, 144, 145, 146, 147
Wickmann 196
Winslow 196
Wizard 147